MARY BAKER EDDY | Speaking for Herself

Publisher's Note

*M*ary Baker Eddy, Speaking for Herself inaugurates a new series of books featuring many of Mary Baker Eddy's heretofore unpublished writings. Offering new perspectives on Mrs. Eddy — her life, her writings, and her enduring achievements — the series aims to enrich readers' understanding of this remarkable woman, who introduced bold new concepts to nineteenth-century society and beyond.

The series draws upon thousands of previously unpublished writings, artifacts, and photographs in The Mary Baker Eddy Collection™. Those who wish to explore the Collection—one of the largest by and about an American woman—can do so firsthand at the Mary Baker Eddy Library for the Betterment of Humanity in Boston, Massachusetts (www.marybakereddylibrary.org).

Mary Baker Eddy, Speaking for Herself is being published at a time when memoirs written by women, particularly women of faith, are something of a book-publishing phenomenon. Popular and scholarly works exploring the experiences of women of various times, places, and cultures are growing in number and diversity, and they are finding an enthusiastic readership. Mrs. Eddy's life experience and spiritual memoirs will no doubt take a prominent place among the recent biographical and spiritual literature by and about women.

This volume contains two autobiographical works by Mary Baker Eddy: *Retrospection and Introspection* and *Footprints Fadeless*. Portions of *Retrospection and Introspection* first appeared as part of a pamphlet in the mid-1880s and was expanded, edited, and then published in its present form in 1891. In contrast, *Footprints Fadeless* is an unfinished and unedited manuscript that Mrs. Eddy composed between 1901 and

1902 largely as a reply to one of her critics. Based on the advice of her lawyers, she chose not to publish it at the time and set it aside for future publication. It is published here in its entirety for the first time, with only minor editing of punctuation and spelling.

The introduction by Jana K. Riess, Religion Book Review Editor for *Publishers Weekly,* places Mary Baker Eddy's autobiographies in historical context, giving a sense of Mrs. Eddy's era and how her life and work were viewed then — and now. Photographs throughout the text and notes at the end of the book provide background information concerning people, places, and issues that Mrs. Eddy touches on but did not explore in depth. In the foreground is a forthright woman, speaking in her own voice, whose message of spiritual healing continues to resonate among men and women today.

MARY BAKER EDDY

Speaking for Herself

AUTOBIOGRAPHICAL REFLECTIONS:

Retrospection and Introspection

Footprints Fadeless

by *[signature: Mary Baker Eddy]*

Discoverer and Founder of Christian Science
Author of *Science and Health with Key to the Scriptures*
Pastor Emeritus, The First Church of Christ, Scientist

THE WRITINGS OF **MaryBakerEddy**

BOSTON

Mary Baker Eddy, Speaking for Herself
Collection, introduction, notes and chronology
© 2002 The Writings of Mary Baker Eddy

Retrospection and Introspection
Copyright, 1891, 1892
by Mary Baker G. Eddy
Copyright renewed, 1919, 1920

Footprints Fadeless
© 2002 The Mary Baker Eddy Collection

Publisher's Cataloging-in-Publication

Eddy, Mary Baker, 1821–1910.
    Mary Baker Eddy, speaking for herself :
autobiographical reflections : retrospection and
introspection : footprints fadeless / by Mary Baker
Eddy. — 1st ed.
    p. cm.
    LCCN 2002111766
    ISBN 0-87952-275-5

    1. Eddy, Mary Baker, 1821-1910. 2. Christian
Scientists—United States—Biography. 3. Christian
Science—History. 4. Spiritual healing—United States—
History. I. Title.

BX6995.E33 2002   289.5'2

FEB 0 6 2007

30

Contents

MARY BAKER EDDY | Speaking for Herself

Introduction

I̲N 1980, drawing upon the fresh energy of the women's movement
and the recent creation of the discipline of women's history, a group
of American historians collaborated on a pioneering volume entitled
Women in American Religion, edited by Janet Wilson James. This foundational collection of essays addressed the role of women in all facets of
history: the rise of Roman Catholic charitable orders, the contributions
of Puritan women in early New England, and the tremendous opportunities that became available to nineteenth-century women in the missionary field. But the essays barely mentioned one of American history's most
significant women — Mary Baker Eddy. She was referred to just twice,
and then only in passing. How could Eddy, who had written a foundational sacred text, founded a new religion, started an international newspaper, and been front-page news at the turn of the century, be relegated to
such a marginal position in a history of women and religion in America?
In 1907, when she was eighty-five years old, *Human Life* magazine declared her "the most famous, interesting, and powerful woman in America, if not the world." Moreover, she had also been the subject of serious
controversy. She was both reviled and revered — sometimes by the same
observer. Mark Twain, for example, called her "the most interesting
woman that ever lived, and the most extraordinary," but he also regarded
her as a "shameless old swindler." [1] In short, Eddy — the object of both
adoration and censure a century ago — is the last person one would have
expected to become a mere footnote in history.

Fortunately, more recent historians and biographers appear to have
discovered her anew. In March 1998, during Women's History Month,
a new exhibit on Mary Baker Eddy opened at the Women's Rights

National Historical Park in Seneca Falls, New York, the birthplace of the women's movement. This temporary exhibit, which continued throughout the sesquicentennial celebration of the Declaration of Sentiments, proved so popular that it became a permanent fixture in the town, and also spawned several other Mary Baker Eddy exhibits that now tour the United States. Eddy had already been inducted into the National Women's Hall of Fame and in 1998 was named by *Religion and Ethics Newsweekly* as one of the top twenty-five most influential religious figures of the twentieth century — one of only three women to be so honored. In 1999, she was recognized by the National Foundation of Women Legislators for her contributions to journalism, and in 2000, she was cited as "one of the leading female religious figures of modern times" in the book *Extraordinary Women: Women Who Changed History.* Clearly, Eddy has been rescued from historical oversight and is now taking her rightful place in the annals of women, religion, and American history.

This renaissance of interest in Mary Baker Eddy comes at a time when her book, *Science and Health with Key to the Scriptures,* is enjoying its strongest sales ever. First published in 1875, *Science and Health* has sold more than ten million copies, a million of which have been purchased in just the last five years. It is now available in thousands of bookstores in more than forty countries. The increased distribution of this book has led to a wider readership, which in turn has generated more interest in the woman who wrote it. Many of the people who read *Science and Health* find that its spiritual teachings enrich their own journeys, whether they are Christian, Jewish, Buddhist, or other.

Why now, nearly a century after her death?

In part, we are becoming more interested in Mary Baker Eddy because we are reconnecting with many of the human elements of her story. Whereas in the nineteenth century her status as a single mother and deserted wife made her an outcast, in our day such circumstances are more likely to cement her popularity as a cause célèbre. Informed by the advances of the women's movement, we are more likely to want to recover Mary Baker Eddy's story as an example of a woman who demonstrated leadership abilities that far exceeded the constraints of her time and place. There is also a Horatio Alger element to her narrative that many people find appealing, even inspiring: here was a woman who pulled herself up by the bootstraps, so to speak, and achieved success, fame, wealth, and presumably great spiritual fulfillment. In our own time, we are likely to resonate with the difficulties of some of her personal circumstances, regarding her as a plucky single mom who overcame poverty and quite resourcefully made her own way in the world. Her personal story could be any of ours, and it inspires us to transcend our circumstances as she did.

On a deeper level, her story speaks to our age's quest for spiritual understanding. The past decade has seen an unprecedented rise in the popularity of books on spirituality and a particular interest in the intersection between body, mind, and spirit. Many in the medical establishment have acknowledged — even encouraged — the pursuit of "alternative" forms of healing to complement medical treatment. In the past decade, for example, approximately fifteen hundred research studies, reviews, articles, and clinical trials have explored the relationship between healing and prayer, and over half of all medical schools in the United States now offer courses on spirituality and healing. The renewed interest in Mary Baker Eddy's ideas makes perfect sense in this context. As individuals undertake the quest for spiritual and physical wholeness, many find practical assistance in *Science and Health,* the book she offered to the world. She wrote in the book's preface that she believed "the time for thinkers" had come. As we stand upon the threshold of the twenty-first century, it is clear that "the time for thinkers" continues.

Mary Baker Eddy in the late 1880s. At this time she was starting to write and publish autobiographical information. *Photograph by W. Shaw Warren.*

A B𝚁ɪᴇꜰ S𝚔ᴇᴛᴄʜ
ᴏꜰ ᴛʜᴇ Lɪꜰᴇ ᴏꜰ M𝚊ʀʏ B𝚊ᴋᴇʀ E𝚍ᴅʏ

Mary Baker Eddy was born Mary Morse Baker on July 16, 1821, in Bow, New Hampshire, the last of six children born to Mark and Abigail Baker. Mark Baker was a strict Congregationalist who, as Eddy later noted, "kept the family in the tightest harness I have ever known."[2] He presided over a fairly prosperous New England farm during Eddy's early childhood. While her father had her respect, her mother had her heart and was the person Mary Baker Eddy loved most in the family. Abigail Baker was, by most accounts, a sensible and kind helpmeet, and possibly an early inspiration for Eddy's later insistence that God should be understood as mother as well as father.

A bookish, reflective girl, Eddy suffered from ill health even in childhood, though claims by hostile biographers that she experienced "hysteric" episodes during this period are unsubstantiated. In December 1843, at the age of twenty-two, she married George Washington Glover, a building contractor, and moved with him to the Carolinas. Tragically, her new husband died of yellow fever just six months later, leaving her practically penniless—and pregnant. This was a dark period in her life, marked by the death of her beloved mother and the remarriage of her father just one year later. During these years, she attempted to earn a living with her pen, publishing poetry, short stories, and essays for local and even a few national periodicals. Although she found writing very enjoyable, it did not pay particularly well. Thus Eddy, with only sporadic income, no husband, and a young son to care for, was forced to rely on the kindness of family and friends. When Mark Baker remarried, one of her sisters offered to take her in but did not extend the invitation to Eddy's boisterous son, George, who was sent to live with another family.

The traditional happy ending to this type of nineteenth-century tale would be for the heroine to marry again, which Eddy did in 1853. However, remarriage did not prove to be the solution to her financial problems; it intensified them. Her husband Daniel Patterson was a largely self-trained New Hampshire dentist and homeopathic practitioner with an eye for other women. His charms were considerable, but he failed to support his wife and didn't provide the promised home for young George. By the time he left Mary Baker Eddy in 1866, they had been drifting apart for some time. She was later granted a divorce on charges of desertion.

During her difficult marriage to Daniel Patterson, Eddy had endured several debilitating illnesses and chronic poor health. Over the years, she had sought cures from traditional "heroic" medical doctors,[3] as well as alternative healers such as homeopaths, dietitians, and proponents of hydropathy, or water cure. In 1862, she consulted a "magnetic healer" by the name of Phineas Parkhurst Quimby and endeavored to learn his methods after she experienced a rapid improvement in her health. In 1866, just two weeks after Quimby's death, Eddy had a serious fall on the ice in Lynn, Massachusetts. Unable to move and in terrible pain, she was told that death was near at hand. Three days after her fall, she read New Testament accounts of Jesus' healings, and to the wonder of all present, she arose from her bed and walked. For her, this event marked the beginning of a "discovery [of] how to be well myself, and how to make others so."[4] She was beginning to recognize her calling as a healer and a teacher.

By 1870, Eddy had begun healing and teaching others — primarily her immediate family and friends, and then strangers who either met her by chance or came to her for healing. She taught her first official class in 1870, and gradually a movement of spiritual seekers united around her leadership. This entry into public life points to the fact that

Mary Baker Eddy inverted the traditional pattern of life for a Victorian woman: as biographer Gillian Gill notes, her halcyon days were not in her teens or early twenties, but in her sixties, seventies, and eighties. She became more, not less, powerful as her life waxed on. She was fifty-four when she published the first edition of *Science and Health*, which would go through a mind-boggling 418 numbered editions (i.e., printings) during her lifetime.[5] Revising and perfecting it was, she felt, her life's work. While completing the first edition of *Science and Health* in 1875, she was for the first time able to rejoice in what Virginia Woolf would call a room of her own: the year that *Science and Health* was published, she was finally able to purchase a small house for herself. To afford the mortgage payments, she rented out many of the rooms but reserved the attic for her own use. There she spent much time writing and reading.

The late 1870s and 1880s were years of tremendous growth for Eddy, who continued revising *Science and Health* and publishing shorter theological works. She founded a college and a journal, gave rousing sermons and speeches in Boston-area pulpits, and began to attract newspaper attention. She also married again in 1877, and by all accounts the third time was the charm: Asa Gilbert Eddy was a devoted husband and loyal student who quietly assisted his wife in all her pursuits. However, these were also trying years; she was involved in prolonged legal battles with several former students and saw her reputation distorted by the press. She was also accused of having stolen key ideas on spiritual healing from her mentor, Phineas Parkhurst Quimby, charges that Eddy vociferously denied but which would dog her all of her life.

In the late 1880s and 1890s, we see Eddy leaving Boston to return to New Hampshire, closing the college she had founded in 1881, disbanding the Christian Scientist Association, and focusing more on her writing.[6]

It was during this period that she published *Retrospection and Introspection,* the most sophisticated and complete of her autobiographical writings, which is included in this volume. Her followers in Boston were engaged in completing a "Mother Church" edifice in 1894 and continued the impressive growth of the movement. On the personal front, however, these were challenging years for Eddy. After her dear husband Asa died in 1882, she became terribly lonely—a woman who, by her later years, was surrounded by students but had no peers. Her loneliness caused her to make at least one fairly disastrous decision about whom she could trust: she overlooked important character flaws in Ebenezer Foster, the man she adopted as her son in 1888. "Benny" turned out to be a poor choice, and Eddy abandoned the relationship by the late 1890s.

As an octogenarian, Eddy showed no sign of diminishing. She moved back to the Boston area in 1908, at the age of eighty-six, and later that year founded *The Christian Science Monitor.* Its motto—"to injure no man, but to bless all mankind"—perhaps is a pointed reference to some of the print attacks she had endured in the last decade of her life. For these denunciations were to be found in some of the nation's most prominent periodicals; *McClure's Magazine* ran a devastating biographical series on Eddy in 1907, and there was widespread coverage of a 1907 lawsuit that Eddy's biological and adopted sons and other petitioners had initiated. They claimed that she was mentally incapacitated and that her estate (now quite considerable) should pass to the petitioners, not to her church. The lawsuit was ultimately dismissed.

Mary Baker Eddy died in her sleep on December 3, 1910, at the age of eighty-nine. Her last written words, formed on a tablet two days before her passing, were "God is my life."[7]

Mary Baker Eddy
in the Nineteenth Century

In the prologue to his 1953 novel *The Go-Between* Leslie Poles Hartley warned his readers that "The past is a foreign country; they do things differently there."[8] Such admonitions bear repeating. It is all too easy to approach Mary Baker Eddy with the perspectives and biases of the early twenty-first century, when such a worldview would indeed be "a foreign country" to Eddy and her contemporaries.

In many ways, particularly theologically, she was indeed years ahead of her time. *Science and Health* was a daring book, one that, as biographer Gillian Gill has concluded, "takes on the great questions of God and man, good and evil, and . . . rejects orthodox verities."[9] Eddy put forth radical ideas: that God was both Father and Mother, that certain passages of the Bible resulted from scribal error or theological misunderstanding, and that scientific prayer could replicate the healings recounted in the Old and New Testaments. She did not accept any passage of the Bible without first dissecting and analyzing it, always uncovering new layers of meaning. She assigned to God's Motherhood a higher plane than God's Fatherhood, since the female was "the last [to be created], therefore the highest idea given of Him."[10] She hit upon a foundational doctrine of Christian Science: that Spirit, not matter, is what is real, despite all appearance to the contrary.

Mary Baker Eddy's theology was also ahead of its time in its emphasis on the connection between mind, body, and spirit. She refused to accept the division between mind and body that was creeping into late-nineteenth-century medical science, supplanting more traditional and integrated methods of healing. Her approach to healing was both physical and theological: bodily healing was a natural result of an understanding of, or alignment with, God. Mary Baker Eddy maintained that a loving, benevolent, perfect God would desire only health and wholeness for all creation. God's children were made in God's image, and that image was good. This is a far cry from the Calvinism of Eddy's own childhood, a theology that had positioned human beings as sinners who were separated from God by a great and terrible chasm. In the Calvinist view, God could transcend that chasm and redeem individual persons from sin — but only if *God* chose to do so. Eddy joined a number of her contemporaries in rejecting Calvinism and claiming that God's children were fundamentally good and free. She also went a step further by asserting that our inherent spiritual nature is *perfect,* not just good, and that the discovery of this spiritual perfection brings about transformation and healing in the human experience.

Although ahead of her time in many ways, Mary Baker Eddy was also very much a product of the nineteenth century. Her views on gender, addressed at some length below, were forged in the fires of Victorian sensibility. Her views on race were also in keeping with the spirit of the times; although she was an abolitionist, she notes in her autobiography *Footprints Fadeless* that she agreed "with the Southrons, as to racial distinctions, such as nature constitutes."[11] In other words, she did not support the enslavement of one human being by another, but she never openly challenged the widely held perception that blacks were inferior to whites (although her teachings do not support this perception).[12]

Mary Baker Eddy's search for more holistic forms of healing is also archetypal for many in her generation. She was not alone in suffering from poor health, nor was she unique in her quest to find healing, even if that search required transcending the limitations of contemporary medical science. Nineteenth-century cures included hydropathy, homeopathy, various diet regimens (the Graham diet and Kellogg vegetarianism being

among the most popular), and magnet therapy. Near the end of the century, the field of chiropractic also attracted many who sought to heal the
body of various diseases. In this complex world of mental healers, homeopaths, and the like, Eddy was unique in her insistence upon the mental
nature and ultimate unreality of illness. Other healers claimed, as she did,
that there was a strong connection between mind and body, but she alone
elevated the discussion from a material plane to a wholly spiritual one.

The "Cult of True Womanhood"

The late nineteenth century was a period that, perhaps more than any
other in American history, prescribed a very set group of characteristics,
acceptable tasks, and values to women. The term "cult of true womanhood" refers to the mid- to late-nineteenth-century sensibility about
women's roles. Theirs was to be a separate sphere, a world apart from the
dangers of commerce and industry. Whereas in the eighteenth century,
when Americans toiled in mostly agrarian, family-based labor, both men
and women were expected to participate fully in the family farm or business, the nineteenth century saw a spurt of industrialization and work created outside the home. Gender roles became quite entrenched for the
middle classes: men were to sally forth into the new industrial world to be
breadwinners, while women were to nurture children and maintain a
quiet sanctity about the home. Industrialization also changed women's
lives. Freed from some of the most tedious chores by the mass production
of many household goods, they could expend their energies instilling religious values in their children and cultivating a spiritual atmosphere in
the home.[13] In effect, the "cult of true womanhood" opened some paths
to women (particularly in the area of religious leadership in the home),
while it closed others.

Of course, the reality wasn't quite that simple, and Eddy's case demonstrates perhaps more clearly than others how nineteenth-century women carefully negotiated their work in the public sphere with expectations that they should remain in the private sphere. In terms of her success and the scope of her influence, Mary Baker Eddy can be compared to only a handful of women of her era—for example, the temperance activist Frances Willard, the novelist Harriet Beecher Stowe, and the British writer Harriet Martineau. In her seventies and eighties, Eddy led a movement that constituted hundreds of thousands of members and was planting branch churches around the world. She had become a wealthy woman solely through her own tireless industry and wise investment of capital. For a woman to succeed so conspicuously in a man's world in the nineteenth century was a bit disreputable. For a woman twice widowed and once divorced, to do so was something approaching a scandal. Yet she was certain that she had earned her success; when a male reporter interviewed her in 1907, she simply stated the facts: "Young man, I made my money with my pen, just as you do, and I have a right to it."[14] Touché.

However, it would be a mistake to categorize Mary Baker Eddy as a radical feminist. During her day, there were numerous women's rights causes afoot, from suffrage to property rights, and she was tangentially involved in only a few of them. At best, scholar Susan Hill Lindley has said, Eddy can be regarded as an "ambiguous" feminist, committed in some ways to the full advancement of women but quite traditional in others.[15] In her writings, some of this traditionalism is apparent in a rather flowery description of her own mother, a eulogy she quotes in full in *Retrospection and Introspection*. Abigail Baker's presence was "like the gentle dew and cheerful light," elevating the conversation and the character of all those who surrounded her. She "was untiring in her efforts to secure the happiness of her family," devoting herself to her children's welfare.[16]

Like most people, Eddy's views on gender reflected a pastiche of stubborn resistance to convention and also a healthy dependence upon it. Perhaps the most radical aspect of the religious movement she founded was its insistence that women, as well as men, were fully responsible for their own health and spiritual well-being. No intercessor in the form of a priest or minister stood between women and the divine Principle; no male doctor was entrusted to effect a miracle cure in the most unfortunate medical cases. Instead, patients could pray for themselves and heal their own illnesses.

Women's religious leadership became a routine force in Christian Science.[17] As Gillian Gill has noted, the fact that women practitioners charged money for their services and were able to make a reasonable living performing valuable work increased their status. They advertised their healing services and had notable success in obstetrics and gynecology, an area that was at that time profoundly underserved by conventional medicine.[18]

THE WRITING OF A LIFE

Mary Baker Eddy's views on gender become even more salient as we consider her mindset in writing an autobiography. The mere existence of female autobiography was brazen and daring during this period; for a woman to make a published record of her life was a rather scandalous exploit. As Jill Ker Conway has noted, "The mere act of sitting down to write an autobiography broke the code of female respectability, because doing so required a woman to believe that her direct experience, rather than her relationships with others, was what gave meaning to her life."[19]

One way that Mary Baker Eddy softens the impact of *Retrospection and Introspection* is to begin it in terms that an audience schooled in the "cult of true womanhood" would understand: her family. Opening with a history of her ancestors, hearth, and home made the whole enterprise of female autobiography somewhat less threatening. In effect, Eddy is attempting to have her cake and eat it too: she has the audacity to write a narrative account of her own life, but she frames it in the comfortable Victorian parameters of family.[20]

Retrospection and Introspection may begin on familiar ground for a nineteenth-century woman's autobiography, but by its middle chapters Eddy is speaking in a strong and authoritative voice. She insists that she alone was responsible for writing and publishing *Science and Health* and records her performance of astounding healings and demonstrations of the truth of Christian Science. The memoir seems to gain in confidence as it progresses; compared to other women's autobiographies of the period, the closing chapters of *Retrospection and Introspection* are nothing short of intrepid. They are, in fact, more theological treatise than autobiography, prompting one to wonder if the "retrospection" promised in the title is confined to the book's first half, which follows the basic contours of traditional autobiography, and the "introspection" takes flight in the book's second half, which reveals Eddy's profound theological mind. One of the final chapters, "Admonition," is particularly striking in its decisive, almost prophetic, voice. Here Eddy has hit her stride and is preaching to the masses. She does not apologize for being a woman who imparts spiritual truth; she just sets it down, gives instructions to her students, and lets the chips fall where they may. The second half of her memoir violates just about every custom of women's autobiography. She is not afraid to be in charge.

In this way, Mary Baker Eddy's autobiographical writing differs quite markedly from other women's memoirs of the period. According to Conway, male autobiographies of the nineteenth century show their authors to be the heroes of their own stories, and active agents in changing the world around them. Women's narratives, by contrast, often show their authors to be the passive recipients of action. Men see themselves as actors, while women typically view themselves as having been acted *upon*. Even so renowned a leader as Jane Addams, founder and director of Hull House in Chicago, used the passive voice throughout her memoir (which, incidentally, she gave the rather distant title of *Twenty Years at Hull House,* thereby making the place, not the person, the star). Conway writes that Addams "deliberately disguised the way she had planned her life. There were probably few women in America of Addams's generation with greater personal agency, but she presents the events of her life as if they had somehow just happened to her."[21] In contrast, Eddy—who, it should be remembered, was constantly defending herself against charges that she had plagiarized her writings—takes responsibility for the success of her writings and her church and takes pains to justify the legitimacy of her calling as a spiritual leader. And, also in contrast to women's autobiographies of the period, her three marriages are almost incidental to the story; the chapter on her third husband, Asa Gilbert Eddy, is just one paragraph long.

That Eddy chose and directed the contents of her autobiography is of paramount importance. An autobiography should not be read primarily as a factual, detailed historical rendering of events or be held to the same standards as "objective" history (if such a discipline can indeed be said to exist). Rather, it is one person's understanding of a life, with experiences carefully selected and presented for public consumption. Why would she include great detail of her successes in healing and building a new religion and very little about her family or home life? Why, also, would some of her accounts of events not coincide exactly with other people's versions?

Gillian Gill has written that Mary Baker Eddy sometimes "showed that tendency to trim the past to suit the needs of the present."[22] Writing *Retrospection and Introspection* at the age of seventy and *Footprints Fadeless* at the age of eighty, long-past events were sometimes forgotten, exaggerated, or downplayed, depending on their importance to her at the time of the writing. Readers of autobiography must always ask themselves some formative questions: At what point in the author's life was the autobiography recorded? What added perspective might later years grant to past events? Might they also distort the reality of what happened?

In most key areas, Eddy's version of events is confirmed by the historical record. For example, anti-Eddy biographers have for years ridiculed her assertion that her son George was "sent away" from her without her consent, to live in Minnesota with the Cheney family. "A plot was consummated for keeping us apart," she claims in *Retrospection and Introspection*.[23] Her detractors have dismissed this conspiracy theory as the lame pretext of an inadequate, uncaring mother, who sent her son away herself so that she could be free of the constraints of motherhood. However, one witness testified later that

> Mrs. Patterson grieved and worried [about young George], because she could not see her child and told the Dr. [Patterson, her husband] that she had given up her folks and had come off up there with him and that she must see the boy and teach him, but Patterson would not let him come near, and without her knowing one day the Cheneys moved away, out west and took the boy.[24]

In this case, then, it would seem that Eddy's own version of events can be regarded as mostly accurate. She did make one small error of fact, however, and this in itself is interesting. She says that George first went to live with the Cheneys when he was just four years of age, when he was actually six. The fact that Eddy remembered her son as younger and more vulnerable than he was at this time perhaps reveals her own anguish over their separation.

In a few cases, however, some distortions did occur. For example, in later years, Eddy tended to highlight her own early antislavery activities, even claiming that she had been an ardent and outspoken abolitionist during the 1844 winter she spent in the South with her first husband. In her account, she "spoke freely against slavery and wrote vigorous articles for the press in favor of freedom," even endangering her personal safety by her blunt abolitionist stance. She also maintained that when her husband died, his wealth was primarily tied up in slaves, but that she eschewed the fortune that would have been hers by selling them and freed them instead, making herself a penniless widow. The historical record does not exactly bear this out.[25] There is no evidence that her first husband was a slaveowner at all (though he probably hired slaves on a contract basis), let alone that Eddy magnanimously freed the slaves upon his death. There is also no proof that she published articles in opposition to slavery in the press. Notably, although she made these claims to various members of her household in conversation, she did not do so in print in any of her autobiographical writings. (*Footprints Fadeless*, in fact, equivocates on the issue of Mr. Glover owning slaves; Eddy writes only that he had been *said* to have "much property" in slaves.)[26]

SPIRITUAL AUTOBIOGRAPHY

Mary Baker Eddy's memoirs are not strictly autobiographical, adhering to the chronological form and factual style of a memoir. Some of her writing—particularly the first half of *Retrospection and Introspection*—belongs within the subgenre of "spiritual autobiography," a classification with a style all its own. Spiritual autobiography requires more than merely ornamenting a traditional autobiography with a few paragraphs about the writer's conversion experience, churchgoing habits, or "dark night of the soul." It often demands, instead, that every fact or incident be interpreted through a spiritual lens. Spiritual autobiography seeks to explain the sometimes complex intersection between a life journey and a faith journey; it makes religion salient to the daily experiences of ordinary people, demonstrating how God can break into human time and personal affairs.

The irony of spiritual autobiography is that its genre specifications sometimes compete with the demands of an ordinary autobiography. In a traditional autobiography, the self is paramount, while in a spiritual autobiography, the self is a tool of the divine, chosen for a divinely appointed mission.[27] Moreover, in traditional autobiography, one's "true" self is often masked by one's public presentation. In spiritual autobiography, that tradition is mitigated by the idea that the spiritual is supposed to cut through all of those public layers and outer shells, revealing the deepest, most authentic self.

Of course, in Eddy's case, those competing ideals are both present. She was ever-conscious of her public role and utilized both of her autobiographies (particularly *Footprints Fadeless*) as opportunities to defend herself against her critics and tell her story on her own terms. There are moments when Eddy's soul shines forth and others when she employs standard autobiographical techniques to carefully craft a persona for the world to see.

In most spiritual autobiographies, the author hearkens back to early childhood experiences as evidence of spiritual calling, or chosenness. Mary Baker Eddy is no exception. In "Voices Not Our Own," the third chapter of *Retrospection and Introspection*, she describes a twelve-month period when she was approximately eight years old, when she

> repeatedly heard a voice, calling me distinctly by name, three times, in an ascending scale. I thought this was my mother's voice, and sometimes went to her, beseeching her to tell me what she wanted. Her answer was always, "Nothing, child! What do you mean?" Then I would say, "Mother, who *did* call me? I heard somebody call *Mary*, three times!"[28]

This voice, calling her name, is reminiscent (as Eddy herself observes) of the biblical account of the prophet Samuel being called by God in his youth (1 Samuel 3). As in the biblical story, Eddy hears a voice calling her three times, supposing it to be the voice of a parent. She eventually comes to realize, as the young Samuel did millennia before her, that it was a calling from God. What is interesting in Eddy's account is that it is a mother, not a father, who recognizes the voice for its true divine import, reading her the account of Samuel and encouraging her to answer as Samuel had: "Speak, Lord; for thy servant heareth." In fact, in Eddy's account, *all* of the people who are associated with the voice are female: her mother, her grandmother, her cousin Mehitable, Eddy, and even the voice itself. Such a reimagination of the Samuel narrative has clear resonances with the theology of Christian Science, which posits a slightly more than coequal maternal aspect of God.

Another early chapter of the memoir also has biblical overtones: when Eddy recounts her examination for candidacy to become a member of the Congregational Church, she gives her age at this examination as twelve years. In point of fact, she was seventeen when she joined the church, a fairly major discrepancy. It is certainly possible that Eddy simply forgot the specifics in the intervening years or that an anachronism had crept into the text—by the end of the nineteenth century, as today, young people joined the church around puberty, not as nearly grown adults, as had been the custom during her childhood.[29] However, it is surely no coincidence that Eddy casts this story in the same terms as the Gospel of Luke, which records Jesus going to the temple at the age of twelve and questioning the elders there. Like Jesus, the young Mary Baker took no creed for granted; in her case, the Calvinist doctrine of predestination had actually caused her such distress that she had been taken with a fever.[30] In her testimony at the examination in church, the young girl's words so impressed and touched the congregation that

> even the oldest church-members wept. After the meeting was over they came and kissed me. To the astonishment of many, the good clergyman's heart also melted, and he received me into their communion, and my protest along with me.[31]

Like the young Jesus, whose words had "astonished" and "amazed" the elders in the temple, Mary Baker electrified the elders of her day. Whether she was twelve years old or seventeen is less important than her self-understanding as she presents it in the autobiography: she was chosen to do great things.

Mary Baker Eddy's autobiographical writings alternate between presenting her spiritual development as gradual or instantaneous. Some of the rhetoric makes her transformation into a great religious leader seem inevitable ("I climbed to the sun-crowned heights of Christian Science through the illumined truths of Holy Writ, and by precept and example").[32] Such statements do not tell us much, as they are cloaked in spiritualized terminology and removed from the hard-won journey of faith. More revealing are statements that demonstrate change over time: "In my revisions of *Science and Health,* its entire keynote has grown steadily clearer, and louder, and sweeter."[33] At one point in *Footprints Fadeless,* she describes her spiritual journey as one of "practical evolution."

> Was Newton capable of satisfactorily stating the laws of gravitation when first he discovered that ponderous principle? Much less could I, at first, formulate and express the infinite Principle and the divine Laws of which God gave me the first faint gleam in my hour of physical agony and mental illumination.[34]

In other words, Eddy acknowledges here that she did not immediately understand the healing after that famous fall on the ice in Lynn. It took years of writing, reading, praying, thinking, and healing before she became certain that she had discovered the full practice of scientific Christianity.

This acknowledgment in *Footprints Fadeless* is as close as Mary Baker Eddy comes to spiritual self-revelation. Spiritual autobiographies often contain a "dark night of the soul"— a crucible experience through which the author passed and which tested and strengthened her faith. One of the most fascinating elements of Eddy's autobiographies is that while she experienced tremendously dark times in her life, her memoirs barely mention them. This may have been because, with the hindsight of decades between herself and the original events, she was able to gloss over any past feelings of depression or despair, knowing that all would have a successful outcome. In May 1857, for example, Eddy was ill with an inflammation of the spine. Although her memoirs make no mention of this illness or the pain and sadness it caused her, she recorded some of her feelings in an early scrapbook. On May 7, she despaired, "Oh! How long must I bear this burden life? This long and lingering passage through darkness and dull decay, uncheered by many of life's last solaces even till now."[35] These words contain a deep, raw melancholy that is unmatched by any reminiscence in her autobiographies. Perhaps the feelings had mellowed with age, or—as is more likely—she simply chose to present her life in terms of her discovery rather than the personal trials she had faced. Clearly, Eddy passed through difficult times — even the proverbial "dark night of the soul." But on such questions her memoirs are largely silent.

RETROSPECTION AND INTROSPECTION

The first, and most complete, of Mary Baker Eddy's memoirs is *Retrospection and Introspection,* published in 1891. She based it on an earlier pamphlet first published in 1885, which contained both autobiographical and theological material; *Retrospection and Introspection* underwent several revisions before it reached its present form. Its publication came over two years after she had stepped back from the day-to-day workings of the movement she had founded: she moved away from Boston, resigned as pastor of the church, closed the Massachusetts Metaphysical College she had founded, and dissolved the Christian Scientist Association. In the intervening time, she had turned toward solitude and devoted more time to her own writing, specifically to a revised and expanded version of *Science and Health*. She relocated to Concord, New Hampshire, a city not far from Bow, her birthplace. It was here, as she gazed out at the New England landscape that had nurtured her spirit, that she weighed and filtered through the events of her life.

All was not peaceful in her heart, however. Reading between the lines of the autobiography, readers can discern an undertone of discord simply in the ways that Eddy defends herself against her critics. In the 1870s and 1880s, she was not nearly as famous as she would become at the turn of the century and therefore had not yet attracted the public opprobrium that would be her burden to bear in her final years. However, as a local and even regional celebrity, she had weathered a few print attacks. Some critics declared her to be a huckster, interested in curing others only for personal gain; to this end she presents herself in *Retrospection and Introspection* as one who from childhood had only sought "diligently for the knowledge of God" in order to assist others.[36] She also offers examples of times she lived on "a small annuity" and refused any payment for her healing services.[37] In like manner, Eddy uses her memoir as an opportunity to defend herself against charges of plagiarizing the writings of Phineas Parkhurst Quimby. In her memoir she claims that others have mistaken *her* writings for Quimby's original work.[38] She distances herself from the ideas of other mental healers and from faith healers, with whom she had sometimes been confused in the public mind.[39] In short, then, Mary Baker Eddy used the autobiography as a sort of plea for normalcy, a chance to answer some of the charges dumped at her door. This is a phenomenon that we will see even more clearly in *Footprints Fadeless*.

By 1891, Eddy was beginning to craft a public persona and to defend herself from external attacks. In *Retrospection and Introspection,* she accomplishes both of these objectives, while wrestling with the appropriateness of her own status as autobiographer. She can almost be regarded as an ambivalent autobiographer, one who saw the need to record her life (particularly as doing so afforded an opportunity to set the record straight), but who also struggled with the sense that a memoir called too much attention to one individual's life. She observed

> Whosoever looks to me personally for his health or holiness, mistakes. He that by reason of human love or hatred or any other cause clings to my material personality, greatly errs, stops his own progress, and loses the path to health, happiness, and heaven. The Scriptures and Christian Science reveal "the way," and personal revelators will take their proper place in history, but will not be deified.[40]

She was afraid that individuals would confuse the message with its messenger and regard her personal life as a sort of entryway into spiritual truth. She therefore approached the writing of her life very, very carefully. As *Retrospection and Introspection* progresses, she moves from conventional autobiography to a spirited defense of some of her actions, culminating in chapters that are almost wholly theological and impersonal. As she writes, "mere historic incidents and personal events are frivolous and of no moment, unless they illustrate the ethics of Truth. To this end, but only to this end, such narrations may be admissible and advisable."[41] In other words, autobiography is all very well, but only insofar as it points to God as Truth with a capital "T."

FOOTPRINTS FADELESS

Although Mary Baker Eddy attempted to step back from the public arena in the late 1880s, she was not immune from controversy and criticism. In 1890, her student Josephine Woodbury garnered much ridicule for Christian Science when she claimed that her illegitimate son had been conceived immaculately by God. She named the boy "Prince of Peace"

Mary Baker Eddy at the turn of the twentieth century. The photograph was taken by Calvin A. Frye, her personal secretary, at Pleasant View, Eddy's home on the outskirts of Concord, New Hampshire.

and claimed him as a second Christ. When Eddy learned of Woodbury's behavior, she was scandalized and irate, but she forgave the transgressor when she appeared to repent and humbly ask forgiveness. Forgiveness was granted, but Woodbury did nothing to change her ways. In 1896 she was at last permanently excommunicated by the Board of Directors of The Mother Church.

Woodbury then launched a full-scale public attack. In 1899, she sued Mary Baker Eddy for libel, claiming that the leader's Communion message had denounced her as the "Babylonish woman" mentioned in the New Testament Book of Revelation.[42] Woodbury's attorney, Frederick Peabody, engineered the court case as a broad assault on Christian Science and its founder. The case was dismissed within a week of the trial's commencement in 1901, and the whole affair was construed as a resounding legal defeat for Josephine Woodbury. But it was hardly a triumph for Mary Baker Eddy, who found her teachings and personal dealings dredged up for public scrutiny. Therefore, *Footprints Fadeless* emerged out of a situation in which Eddy had just spent two years seeing her movement torn apart in the press and dissected in the courts.

Moreover, the Woodbury-Peabody saga did not end with the dismissal of the libel suit. Frederick Peabody took his case to the court of public opinion, speaking in Boston's Tremont Temple on August 1, 1901. The lecture, which included a full complement of accusations against Eddy, proved popular enough that it was reprinted as a pamphlet, entitled *Complete Exposé of Eddyism or Christian Science, and The Plain Truth Regarding Mary Baker G. Eddy, Founder of Christian Science,* which sold for a quarter.

One of the pamphlet's readers was likely Mary Baker Eddy herself. In the pages of *Footprints Fadeless,* she never mentions Peabody by name but uses her own manuscript to refute many of his specific charges.

Whereas he accused her of once plagiarizing a sermon from her editor, Rev. James Henry Wiggin, Eddy makes a point of noting that she "never preached a sermon of his [Wiggin's]" or passed off his work as her own.[43] In answer to Peabody's claim that Eddy abhorred marriage for her followers and was responsible for tearing families apart, she includes an entire chapter in *Footprints Fadeless* with the pointed title "Marriage Not Prohibited."[44] Another chapter reprints a letter from her secretary, Calvin A. Frye, in which he refutes several of Peabody's other claims: that Eddy was an avaricious fraud, that she had never practiced any philanthropic giving, and — most preposterously — that Frye and Eddy were secretly married.[45] Other indictments are speedily refuted in *Footprints Fadeless,* from the personal (that Eddy cared so little about her first husband that she allowed his body to rot away in an unmarked grave)[46] to the doctrinal (that Eddy conceived of herself as a second Christ and encouraged her followers to worship her).[47] Overall, Eddy sought to repudiate Peabody's statement that she was "the most audacious and most successful adventuress, the most mercenary and calculating charlatan, the most vindictive, relentless and cruel woman the enlightened centuries have produced."[48]

Given this situation, as an autobiography *Footprints Fadeless* is a defensive, wary document, overly prone to affidavits and external proofs that demonstrated the ludicrousness of some of the charges against Mary Baker Eddy. Whereas *Retrospection and Introspection* begins by establishing Eddy's genealogical and spiritual *bona fides* but then moves on, *Footprints Fadeless* is entirely subsumed with authenticating her leadership and her teachings. Thus we see her include a letter from Civil War general Benjamin Butler, which seems to exist in the manuscript for no other reason than to demonstrate a personal connection between the two luminaries. An affidavit from her sister-in-law, Mary Ann Cook Baker, testifies to Mary Baker Eddy's character, and a certificate of ordination is reproduced to demonstrate her spiritual authority. And so on. As Eddy sought to come to terms with her life at the time of this writing, self-defense was clearly uppermost in her mind.

It is because *Footprints Fadeless* is so defensive, so unrelentingly self-protective, that it was never published in the first place.[49] After the protracted and bitter legal dispute with Woodbury, Eddy's attorneys were extremely wary about her publishing a memoir that was, in effect, an instrument of self-defense meant to counter public accusations. After Eddy completed the draft, her legal team advised her to be very cautious about publishing it, lest she risk another lawsuit. "The one thing to be avoided is saying anything that would <u>result in another libel case against her</u>," her attorney admonished.[50] In particular, the attorney recommended avoiding all overt references to Frederick Peabody:

> Certainly <u>Peabody</u> ought not to be mentioned by name. He is not entitled to the distinction of being directly replied to. I can see that there may be great difficulty in replying to the various charges without apparent reference to what he has said, as he probably has said everything. . . . I should advise off-hand, a reply—since Mrs. Eddy has determined that some reply must be made—to the things contained in the *Providence Journal,* ignoring Peabody and his lecture altogether if possible. The reply cannot be couched in too dignified terms.[51]

This letter makes it clear that *Footprints Fadeless* was intended as some sort of response to Peabody's allegations, since Eddy had determined that "some reply must be made." But it was too incendiary to appear in print without instigating further problems. The manuscript was preserved for possible future publication after her attorneys advised her not to publish it, but Eddy never returned to it. It exists here in its original form, untouched for a century. It is more an outline or a skeleton of a book than a coherent, cohesive package. Whereas *Retrospection and Introspection* is very stylized, almost overedited, *Footprints Fadeless* shows Mary Baker Eddy in wholly unvarnished prose. In this unformed autobiographical fragment, Eddy jumps from one topic to the next without transitions, begins defending herself on issues she has not yet explained to the reader, and provides almost no historical background for many of the events she describes. It could even be said that this is not autobiography per se; its format, in fact, is quite similar to *No and Yes,* a question-and-answer pamphlet about Christian Science. In *No and Yes,* Eddy answered some of the questions that had been raised in the press ("Is Christian Science Pantheistic?" "Is Christian Science Blasphemous?" "Should Christians Beware of Christian Science?"). Using short, topical chapters, Eddy attempted to clear up misunderstandings and present her point of view. *Footprints Fadeless* has a very similar raison d'être, not to mention a comparable format.

As an unedited manuscript, *Footprints Fadeless* makes for a difficult read, but the distinct advantage this inchoate form affords us is that it presents the opportunity to see its author at her most unguarded. She has not yet edited out her anger; she offers herself more fully to the reader. Thus we see her elucidating, more extensively than she ever had in print, the gradual *process* by which she came to understand the principles that she illuminated in *Science and Health*. Hers was not an instantaneous epiphany but a spiritual evolution and progressive understanding.[52] She also admits to some of her own shortcomings, calling herself "stern and uncompromising in rebuking sin" though not prone to ill temper or vengeance.[53] She makes the important clarification that she regards "Christ as divine, and myself as a human being seeking Christ."[54] She is, in short, more humanly accessible than ever before.

Footprints Fadeless appears to be a document addressed to two very different audiences simultaneously: the critics who vilified and persecuted Mary Baker Eddy, dredging up old charges that demanded refutation, and her own followers, who often tended too far in the opposite direction by deifying their religion's founder. The autobiography attempts (albeit in a primitive way) to chart a middle course, sharply refuting critics on the one hand, but on the other, gently reminding believers of their leader's human limitations. Throughout her later years, Eddy was anxious that her followers should avoid the dangers of "personality," or the tendency to transfer their zeal to her rather than to Christian Science. We see Eddy's reluctance to draw attention to herself in her decline of the Board of Directors' 1895 offer to become Pastor of the newly constructed church in Boston. Eddy (in a letter that is reproduced in *Footprints Fadeless*) politely refused this honor and directed their attention to her magnum opus, *Science and Health*. "Through my book, your textbook, I already speak to you each Sunday," she explained.[55] (The Board did follow her suggestion, offered in the same letter, that she be appointed "Pastor Emeritus.")

Mary Baker Eddy used the pages of *Footprints Fadeless* to remind her followers to resist the temptation of apotheosis of their leader: "Human deification or worship I abjure, as all know who have a true knowledge of me," she insisted.[56] She had already taken pains, in her revisions of *Science and Health,* to divest that book of much of its autobiographical content. The spiritual message, not the traits or personal experience of the author, would become its hallmark. She wrote in the early 1890s that

> In the flesh I am not what I desire to be; I am not what imagination would make me. I am not a heathen concept nor idol. I am not a personality to which others look and are saved, and the world's present

ignorance of the place I occupy should suspend its judgment. I am not the Door through which to enter, nor the Rock whereon to build, but what God has spoken to this age through me is the <u>way</u> and <u>sure foundation</u>, and no man entereth by any other way into Christian Science.[57]

In this way, Mary Baker Eddy deflected adulation from herself and redirected attention to the ideas that, she claimed, God had spoken through her.

Eddy's autobiographical writings offer a unique perspective on the woman who so persistently enlarged the boundaries of spirituality, womanhood, and medicine more than a century ago. She was a unique, strong, and visionary leader, a product of the nineteenth century who nevertheless looked into the future and claimed its progress. "I have faced the destiny of a discoverer and pioneer from first to last," she wrote in *Footprints Fadeless*.[58] As a spiritual pilgrim and leader, her footprints are surely fadeless.

—JANA K. RIESS

Retrospection and Introspection

by MARY BAKER EDDY

Ancestral Shadows

My ancestors, according to the flesh, were from both Scotland and England, my great-grandfather, on my father's side, being John McNeil of Edinburgh.

His wife, my great-grandmother, was Marion Moor, and her family is said to have been in some way related to Hannah More, the pious and popular English authoress of a century ago.

I remember reading, in my childhood, certain manuscripts containing Scriptural sonnets, besides other verses and enigmas which my grandmother said were written by my great-grandmother. But because my great-grandmother wrote a stray sonnet and an occasional riddle, it was no sign that she inherited a spark from Hannah More, or was her relative.

John and Marion Moor McNeil had a daughter, who perpetuated her mother's name. This second Marion McNeil in due time was married to an Englishman, named Joseph Baker, and so became my paternal grandmother, the Scotch and English elements thus mingling in her children.

Mrs. Marion McNeil Baker was reared among the Scotch Covenanters, and had in her character that sturdy Calvinistic devotion to Protestant liberty which gave those religionists the poetic daring and pious picturesqueness which we find so graphically set forth in the pages of Sir Walter Scott and in John Wilson's sketches.

Joseph Baker and his wife, Marion McNeil, came to America seeking "freedom to worship God;" though they could hardly have crossed the Atlantic more than a score of years prior to the Revolutionary period.

With them they brought to New England a heavy sword, encased in a brass scabbard, on which was inscribed the name of a kinsman upon whom the weapon had been bestowed by Sir William Wallace, from

The farmhouse in Bow, New Hampshire, where Mary Baker was born in 1821. This photograph shows the condition of the building in about 1907, after it had been altered and moved. It was destroyed by fire in 1910.

whose patriotism and bravery comes that heart-stirring air, "Scots wha hae wi' Wallace bled."

My childhood was also gladdened by one of my Grandmother Baker's books, printed in olden type and replete with the phraseology current in the seventeenth and eighteenth centuries.

Among grandmother's treasures were some newspapers, yellow with age. Some of these, however, were not very ancient, nor had they crossed the ocean; for they were American newspapers, one of which contained a full account of the death and burial of George Washington.

A relative of my Grandfather Baker was General Henry Knox of Revolutionary fame. I was fond of listening, when a child, to grandmother's stories about General Knox, for whom she cherished a high regard.

In the line of my Grandmother Baker's family was the late Sir John Macneill, a Scotch knight, who was prominent in British politics, and at one time held the position of ambassador to Persia.[59]

My grandparents were likewise connected with Capt. John Lovewell of Dunstable, New Hampshire, whose gallant leadership and death, in the Indian troubles of 1722-1725, caused that prolonged contest to be known historically as Lovewell's War.

A cousin of my grandmother was John Macneil, the New Hampshire general who fought at Lundy's Lane, and won distinction in 1814 at the neighboring battle of Chippewa, towards the close of the War of 1812.

Autobiographic Reminiscences

This venerable grandmother had thirteen children, the youngest of whom was my father, Mark Baker, who inherited the homestead, and with his brother, James Baker, he inherited my grandfather's farm of about five hundred acres, lying in the adjoining towns of Concord and Bow, in the State of New Hampshire.

One hundred acres of the old farm are still cultivated and owned by Uncle James Baker's grandson, brother of the Hon. Henry Moore Baker of Washington, D.C.[60]

The farm-house, situated on the summit of a hill, commanded a broad picturesque view of the Merrimac River and the undulating lands of three townships. But change has been busy. Where once stretched broad fields of bending grain waving gracefully in the sunlight, and orchards of apples, peaches, pears, and cherries shone richly in the mellow hues of autumn, — now the lone night-bird cries, the crow caws cautiously, and wandering winds sigh low requiems through dark pine groves. Where green pastures bright with berries, singing brooklets, beautiful wild flowers, and flecked with large flocks and herds, covered areas of rich acres, — now the scrub-oak, poplar, and fern flourish.

The wife of Mark Baker was Abigail Barnard Ambrose, daughter of Deacon Nathaniel Ambrose of Pembroke, a small town situated near Concord, just across the bridge, on the left bank of the Merrimac River.

Grandfather Ambrose was a very religious man, and gave the money for erecting the first Congregational Church in Pembroke.

In the Baker homestead at Bow I was born, the youngest of my parents' six children and the object of their tender solicitude.

During my childhood my parents removed to Tilton, eighteen miles from Concord, and there the family remained until the names of both father and mother were inscribed on the stone memorials in the Park Cemetery of that beautiful village.

My father possessed a strong intellect and an iron will. Of my mother I cannot speak as I would, for memory recalls qualities to which the pen can never do justice. The following is a brief extract from the eulogy of the Rev. Richard S. Rust, D.D., who for many years had resided in Tilton and knew my sainted mother in all the walks of life.

> The character of Mrs. Abigail Ambrose Baker was distinguished for numerous excellences. She possessed a strong intellect, a sympathizing heart, and a placid spirit. Her presence, like the gentle dew and cheerful light, was felt by all around her. She gave an elevated character to

the tone of conversation in the circles in which she moved, and directed attention to themes at once pleasing and profitable.

As a mother, she was untiring in her efforts to secure the happiness of her family. She ever entertained a lively sense of the parental obligation, especially in regard to the education of her children. The oft-repeated impressions of that sainted spirit, on the hearts of those especially entrusted to her watch-care, can never be effaced, and can hardly fail to induce them to follow her to the brighter world. Her life was a living illustration of Christian faith.

My childhood's home I remember as one with the open hand. The needy were ever welcome, and to the clergy were accorded special household privileges.

Among the treasured reminiscences of my much respected parents, brothers, and sisters, is the memory of my second brother, Albert Baker, who was, next to my mother, the very dearest of my kindred. To speak of his beautiful character as I cherish it, would require more space than this little book can afford.

My brother Albert was graduated at Dartmouth College in 1834, and was reputed one of the most talented, close, and thorough scholars ever connected with that institution. For two or three years he read law at Hillsborough, in the office of Franklin Pierce, afterwards

Mark Baker, the father of Mary Baker Eddy, date unknown. From a visiting card in Eddy's photograph album.

President of the United States; but later Albert spent a year in the office of the Hon. Richard Fletcher of Boston. He was consequently admitted to the bar in two States, Massachusetts and New Hampshire. In 1837 he succeeded to the law-office which Mr. Pierce had occupied, and was soon elected to the Legislature of his native State, where he served the public interests faithfully for two consecutive years. Among other important bills which were carried through the Legislature by his persistent energy was one for the abolition of imprisonment for debt.

In 1841 he received further political preferment, by nomination to Congress on a majority vote of seven thousand, — it was the largest vote of the State; but he passed away at the age of thirty-one, after a short illness, before his election. His noble political antagonist, the Hon. Isaac Hill, of Concord, wrote of my brother as follows: —

> Albert Baker was a young man of uncommon promise. Gifted with the highest order of intellectual powers, he trained and schooled them by intense and almost incessant study throughout his short life. He was fond of investigating abstruse and metaphysical principles, and he never forsook them until he had explored their every nook and corner, however hidden and remote. Had life and health been spared to him, he would have made himself one of the most distinguished men in the country. As a lawyer he was able and learned, and in the successful practice of a very large business. He was noted for his boldness and firmness, and for his powerful advocacy of the side he deemed right. His death will be deplored, with the most poignant grief, by a large number of friends, who expected no more than they realized from his talents and acquirements. This sad event will not be soon forgotten. It blights too many hopes; it carries with it too much of sorrow and loss. It is a public calamity.

Voices Not Our Own

Many peculiar circumstances and events connected with my childhood throng the chambers of memory. For some twelve months, when I was about eight years old, I repeatedly heard a voice, calling me distinctly by name, three times, in an ascending scale. I thought this was my mother's voice, and sometimes went to her, beseeching her to tell me what she wanted. Her answer was always, "Nothing, child! What do you mean?" Then I would say, "Mother, who *did* call me? I heard somebody call *Mary*, three times!" This continued until I grew discouraged, and my mother was perplexed and anxious.

One day, when my cousin, Mehitable Huntoon, was visiting us, and I sat in a little chair by her side, in the same room with grandmother,— the call again came, so loud that Mehitable heard it, though I had ceased to notice it. Greatly surprised, my cousin turned to me and said, "Your mother is calling you!" but I answered not, till again the same call was thrice repeated. Mehitable then said sharply, "Why don't you go? your mother is calling you!" I then left the room, went to my mother, and once more asked her if she had summoned me? She answered as always before. Then I earnestly declared my cousin had heard the voice, and said that mother wanted me. Accordingly she returned with me to grandmother's room, and led my cousin into an adjoining apartment. The door was ajar, and I listened with bated breath. Mother told Mehitable all about this mysterious voice, and asked if she really did hear Mary's name pronounced in audible tones. My cousin answered quickly, and emphasized her affirmation.

That night, before going to rest, my mother read to me the Scriptural narrative of little Samuel, and bade me, when the voice called again, to reply as he did, "Speak, Lord; for Thy servant heareth." The voice came; but I was afraid, and did not answer. Afterward I wept, and prayed that God would forgive me, resolving to do, next time, as my mother had bidden me. When the call came again I did answer, in the words of Samuel, but never again to the material senses was that mysterious call repeated.

> Is it not much that I may worship him,
>   With naught my spirit's breathings to control,
> And feel His presence in the vast and dim
>   And whispering woods, where dying thunders roll
> From the far cataracts? Shall I not rejoice
> That I have learned at last to know His voice
>   From man's? — I will rejoice! My soaring soul
> Now hath redeemed her birthright of the day,
> And won, through clouds, to Him, her own unfettered way!
>
> —Mrs. Hemans

Early Studies

My father was taught to believe that my brain was too large for my body and so kept me much out of school, but I gained book-knowledge with far less labor than is usually requisite. At ten years of age I was as familiar with Lindley Murray's *Grammar*[61] as with the Westminster Catechism; and the latter I had to repeat every Sunday.[62] My favorite studies were natural philosophy, logic, and moral science. From my brother Albert I received lessons in the ancient tongues, Hebrew, Greek, and Latin. My brother studied Hebrew during his college vacations. After

Woodman Sanbornton Academy, Sanbornton, New Hampshire. Mary Baker attended the Woodman Sanbornton Academy and the Sanbornton Academy. Dyer H. Sanborn, mentioned in *Footprints Fadeless*, taught at both. Photograph from the 1930s.

my discovery of Christian Science, most of the knowledge I had gleaned from schoolbooks vanished like a dream.

Learning was so illumined, that grammar was eclipsed. Etymology was divine history, voicing the idea of God in man's origin and significa-tion. Syntax was spiritual order and unity. Prosody, the song of angels, and no earthly or inglorious theme.

Girlhood Composition

From childhood I was a verse-maker. Poetry suited my emotions better than prose. The following is one of my girlhood productions.

ALPHABET AND BAYONET

If fancy plumes aerial flight,
    Go fix thy restless mind
On learning's lore and wisdom's might,
    And live to bless mankind.
The sword is sheathed, 't is freedom's hour,
    No despot bears misrule,
Where knowledge plants the foot of power
    In our God-blessed free school.

Forth from this fount the streamlets flow,
    That widen in their course.
Hero and sage arise to show
    Science the mighty source,
And laud the land whose talents rock
    The cradle of her power,
And wreaths are twined round Plymouth Rock,
    From erudition's bower.

Farther than feet of chamois fall,
    Free as the generous air,
Strains nobler far than clarion call
    Wake freedom's welcome, where

Minerva's silver sandals still
　　Are loosed, and not effete;
Where echoes still my day-dreams thrill,
　　Woke by her fancied feet.

Theological Reminiscence

At the age of twelve I was admitted to the Congregational (Trinitarian) Church,[63] my parents having been members of that body for a half-century. In connection with this event, some circumstances are noteworthy. Before this step was taken, the doctrine of unconditional election, or predestination, greatly troubled me; for I was unwilling to be saved, if my brothers and sisters were to be numbered among those who were doomed to perpetual banishment from God. So perturbed was I by the thoughts aroused by this erroneous doctrine, that the family doctor was summoned, and pronounced me stricken with fever.

My father's relentless theology emphasized belief in a final judgment-day, in the danger of endless punishment, and in a Jehovah merciless towards unbelievers; and of these things he now spoke, hoping to win me from dreaded heresy.

My mother, as she bathed my burning temples, bade me lean on God's love, which would give me rest, if I went to Him in prayer, as I was wont to do, seeking His guidance. I prayed; and a soft glow of ineffable joy came over me. The fever was gone, and I rose and dressed myself, in a normal condition of health. Mother saw this, and was glad. The physician marvelled; and the "horrible decree" of predestination—as John Calvin rightly called his own tenet—forever lost its power over me.[64]

When the meeting was held for the examination of candidates for membership, I was of course present. The pastor was an old-school expounder of the strictest Presbyterian doctrines. He was apparently as eager to have unbelievers in these dogmas lost, as he was to have elect believers converted and rescued from perdition; for both salvation and condemnation depended, according to his views, upon the good pleasure of infinite Love. However, I was ready for his doleful questions, which I answered without a tremor, declaring that never could I unite with the church, if assent to this doctrine was essential thereto.

Distinctly do I recall what followed. I stoutly maintained that I was willing to trust God, and take my chance of spiritual safety with my brothers and sisters, — not one of whom had then made any profession of religion, — even if my creedal doubts left me outside the doors. The minister then wished me to tell him when I had experienced a change of heart; but tearfully I had to respond that I could not designate any precise time. Nevertheless, he persisted in the assertion that I *had* been truly regenerated, and asked me to say how I felt when the new light dawned within me. I replied that I could only answer him in the words of the Psalmist: "Search me, O God, and know my heart: try me, and know my thoughts: and see if there be any wicked way in me, and lead me in the way everlasting."

This was so earnestly said, that even the oldest church-members wept. After the meeting was over they came and kissed me. To the astonishment of many, the good clergyman's heart also melted, and he received me into their communion, and my protest along with me. My connection with this religious body was retained till I founded a church of my own, built on the basis of Christian Science, "Jesus Christ himself being the chief corner-stone."

In confidence of faith, I could say in David's words, "I will go in the

Old North Church, Concord, New Hampshire. This is one of the Congregational churches that the young Mary Baker attended with her family. Illustration from volume 2 of the *History of Concord, New Hampshire, from the Original Grant in Seventeen hundred and twenty-five to the Opening of the Twentieth Century*, edited by James O. Lyford, 1903.

strength of the Lord God: I will make mention of Thy righteousness, even of Thine only. O God, Thou hast taught me from my youth: and hitherto have I declared Thy wondrous works." (Psalms lxxi. 16, 17.)

In the year 1878 I was called to preach in Boston at the Baptist Tabernacle of Rev. Daniel C. Eddy, D.D.,— by the pastor of this church. I accepted the invitation and commenced work.

The congregation so increased in number the pews were not sufficient to seat the audience and benches were used in the aisles. At the close of my engagement we parted in Christian fellowship, if not in full unity of doctrine.

Our last vestry meeting was made memorable by eloquent addresses from persons who feelingly testified to having been healed through my preaching. Among other diseases cured they specified cancers. The cases described had been treated and given over by physicians of the popular schools of medicine, but I had not heard of these cases till the persons who divulged their secret joy were healed. A prominent churchman agreeably informed the congregation that many others present had been healed under my preaching, but were too timid to testify in public.

One memorable Sunday afternoon, a soprano,— clear, strong, sympathetic,— floating up from the pews, caught my ear. When the meeting was over, two ladies pushing their way through the crowd reached the platform. With tears of joy flooding her eyes— for she was a mother— one of them said, "Did you hear my daughter sing? Why, she has not sung before since she left the choir and was in consumption! When she entered this church one hour ago she could not speak a loud word, and now, oh, thank God, she is healed!"

It was not an uncommon occurrence in my own church for the sick to be healed by my sermon. Many pale cripples went into the church leaning on crutches who went out carrying them on their shoulders. "And these signs shall follow them that believe."

The charter for The Mother Church in Boston was obtained June, 1879,[65] and the same month the members, twenty-six in number, extended a call to Mary B. G. Eddy to become their pastor. She accepted the call, and was ordained A.D. 1881.

The Country-seat

Written in youth, while visiting a family friend in the beautiful suburbs of Boston.

Wild spirit of song,— midst the zephyrs at play
In bowers of beauty,— I bend to thy lay,
And woo, while I worship in deep sylvan spot,
The Muses' soft echoes to kindle the grot.
Wake chords of my lyre, with musical kiss,
To vibrate and tremble with accents of bliss.

Here morning peers out, from her crimson repose,
On proud Prairie Queen and the modest Moss-rose;
And vesper reclines— when the dewdrop is shed
On the heart of the pink— in its odorous bed;
But Flora has stolen the rainbow and sky,
To sprinkle the flowers with exquisite dye.

Here fame-honored hickory rears his bold form,
And bares a brave breast to the lightning and storm,
While palm, bay, and laurel, in classical glee,
Chase tulip, magnolia, and fragrant fringe-tree;
And sturdy horse-chestnut for centuries hath given
Its feathery blossom and branches to heaven.

Here is life! Here is youth! Here the poet's world-wish,—
Cool waters at play with the gold-gleaming fish;

While cactus a mellower glory receives
From light colored softly by blossom and leaves;
And nestling alder is whispering low,
In lap of the pear-tree, with musical flow.[*]

Dark sentinel hedgerow is guarding repose,
Midst grotto and songlet and streamlet that flows
Where beauty and perfume from buds burst away,
And ope their closed cells to the bright, laughing day;
Yet, dwellers in Eden, earth yields you her tear,—
Oft plucked for the banquet, but laid on the bier.

Earth's beauty and glory delude as the shrine
Or fount of real joy and of visions divine;
But hope, as the eaglet that spurneth the sod,
May soar above matter, to fasten on God,
And freely adore all His spirit hath made,
Where rapture and radiance and glory ne'er fade.

Oh, give me the spot where affection may dwell
In sacred communion with home's magic spell!
Where flowers of feeling are fragrant and fair,
And those we most love find a happiness rare;
But clouds are a presage,— they darken my lay:
This life is a shadow, and hastens away.

[*]An alder growing from the bent branch of a pear-tree.

Marriage and Parentage

In 1843 I was united to my first husband, Colonel George Washington Glover[66] of Charleston, South Carolina, the ceremony taking place under the paternal roof in Tilton.

After parting with the dear home circle I went with him to the South; but he was spared to me for only one brief year. He was in Wilmington, North Carolina, on business, when the yellow-fever raged in that city, and was suddenly attacked by this insidious disease, which in his case proved fatal.

My husband was a freemason, being a member in Saint Andrew's Lodge, Number 10, and of Union Chapter, Number 3, of Royal Arch masons. He was highly esteemed and sincerely lamented by a large circle of friends and acquaintances, whose kindness and sympathy helped to support me in this terrible bereavement. A month later I returned to New Hampshire, where, at the end of four months, my babe was born.

Colonel Glover's tender devotion to his young bride was remarked by all observers. With his parting breath he gave pathetic directions to his brother masons about accompanying her on her sad journey to the North. Here it is but justice to record, they performed their obligations most faithfully.

After returning to the paternal roof I lost all my husband's property, except what money I had brought with me; and remained with my parents until after my mother's decease.

A few months before my father's second marriage, to Mrs. Elizabeth Patterson Duncan, sister of Lieutenant-Governor George W. Patterson of New York, my little son, about four years of age, was sent away from me,[67] and put under the care of our family nurse, who had married,

George Washington Glover, the son of Mary Baker Eddy, at the time of his service in the Union army during the Civil War.

and resided in the northern part of New Hampshire. I had no training for self-support, and my home I regarded as very precious. The night before my child was taken from me, I knelt by his side throughout the dark hours, hoping for a vision of relief from this trial. The following lines are taken from my poem, "Mother's Darling," written after this separation:—

> Thy smile through tears, as sunshine o'er the sea,
>   Awoke new beauty in the surge's roll!
> Oh, life is dead, bereft of all, with thee,—
>   Star of my earthly hope, babe of my soul.

My second marriage was very unfortunate, and from it I was compelled to ask for a bill of divorce, which was granted me in the city of Salem, Massachusetts.[68]

My dominant thought in marrying again was to get back my child, but after our marriage his stepfather was not willing he should have a home with me. A plot was consummated for keeping us apart. The family to whose care he was committed very soon removed to what was then regarded as the Far West.

After his removal a letter was read to my little son, informing him that his mother was dead and buried. Without my knowledge a guardian was appointed him, and I was then informed that my son was lost. Every means within my power was employed to find him, but without success. We never met again until he had reached the age of thirty-four, had a wife and two children, and by a strange providence had learned that his mother still lived, and came to see me in Massachusetts.

Meanwhile he had served as a volunteer throughout the war for the Union, and at its expiration was appointed United States Marshal of the Territory of Dakota.

It is well to know, dear reader, that our material, mortal history is but the record of dreams, not of man's real existence, and the dream has no place in the Science of being. It is "as a tale that is told," and "as the shadow when it declineth." The heavenly intent of earth's shadows is to chasten the affections, to rebuke human consciousness and turn it gladly from a material, false sense of life and happiness, to spiritual joy and true estimate of being.

The awakening from a false sense of life, substance, and mind in matter, is as yet imperfect; but for those lucid and enduring lessons of Love which tend to this result, I bless God.

Mere historic incidents and personal events are frivolous and of no moment, unless they illustrate the ethics of Truth. To this end, but only to this end, such narrations may be admissible and advisable; but if spiritual conclusions are separated from their premises, the *nexus* is lost, and the argument, with its rightful conclusions, becomes correspondingly obscure. The human history needs to be revised, and the material record expunged.

The Gospel narratives bear brief testimony even to the life of our great Master. His spiritual noumenon and phenomenon silenced portraiture. Writers less wise than the apostles essayed in the Apocryphal New Testament a legendary and traditional history of the early life of Jesus. But St. Paul summarized the character of Jesus as the model of Christianity, in these words: "Consider him that endured such contradiction of sinners against himself." "Who for the joy that was set before him endured the cross, despising the shame, and is set down at the right hand of the throne of God."

It may be that the mortal life-battle still wages, and must continue till its involved errors are vanquished by victory-bringing Science; but this triumph will come! God is over all. He alone is our origin, aim, and being. The real man is not of the dust, nor is he ever created through the flesh; for his father and mother are the one Spirit, and his brethren are all the children of one parent, the eternal good.

Emergence into Light

The trend of human life was too eventful to leave me undisturbed in the illusion that this so-called life could be a real and abiding rest. All things earthly must ultimately yield to the irony of fate, or else be merged into the one infinite Love.

As these pungent lessons became clearer, they grew sterner. Previously the cloud of mortal mind seemed to have a silver lining; but now it was not even fringed with light. Matter was no longer spanned with its rainbow of promise. The world was dark. The oncoming hours were indicated by no floral dial. The senses could not prophesy sunrise or starlight.

Thus it was when the moment arrived of the heart's bridal to more spiritual existence. When the door opened, I was waiting and watching; and, lo, the bridegroom came! The character of the Christ was illuminated by the midnight torches of Spirit. My heart knew its Redeemer. He whom my affections had diligently sought was as the One "altogether lovely," as "the chiefest," the only, "among ten thousand." Soulless famine had fled. Agnosticism, pantheism, and theosophy were void. Being was beautiful, its substance, cause, and currents were God and His idea. I had touched the hem of Christian Science.

The Great Discovery

It was in Massachusetts, in February, 1866, and after the death of the magnetic doctor, Mr. P. P. Quimby,[69] whom spiritualists would associate therewith, but who was in no wise connected with this event, that I discovered the Science of divine metaphysical healing which I afterwards named Christian Science. The discovery came to pass in this way. During twenty years prior to my discovery I had been trying to trace all physical effects to a mental cause; and in the latter part of 1866 I gained the scientific certainty that all causation was Mind, and every effect a mental phenomenon.

Mrs. Mary M. Patterson, of Swampscott, fell upon the ice near the corner of Market and Oxford streets, on Thursday evening, and was severely injured. She was taken up in an insensible condition and carried to the residence of S. M. Bubier, Esq., near by, where she was kindly cared for during the night. Dr. Cushing, who was called, found her injuries to be internal, and of a very serious nature, inducing spasms and intense suffering. She was removed to her home in Swampscott yesterday afternoon, though in a very critical condition.

Item from the *Lynn Reporter*, Saturday, February 3, 1866. This clipping from one of Mary Baker Eddy's scrapbooks describes her fall on the ice on February 1, 1866, at the corner of Market and Oxford Streets in Lynn, Massachusetts.

My immediate recovery from the effects of an injury caused by an accident, an injury that neither medicine nor surgery could reach, was the falling apple that led me to the discovery how to be well myself, and how to make others so.

Even to the homoeopathic physician who attended me, and rejoiced in my recovery, I could not then explain the *modus* of my relief. I could only assure him that the divine Spirit had wrought the miracle— a miracle which later I found to be in perfect scientific accord with divine law.

I then withdrew from society about three years,— to ponder my mission, to search the Scriptures, to find the Science of Mind that should take the things of God and show them to the creature, and reveal the great curative Principle,— Deity.

The Bible was my textbook. It answered my questions as to how I was healed; but the Scriptures had to me a new meaning, a new tongue. Their spiritual signification appeared; and I apprehended for the first time, in their spiritual meaning, Jesus' teaching and demonstration, and the Principle and rule of spiritual Science and metaphysical healing,— in a word, Christian Science.

I named it *Christian*, because it is compassionate, helpful, and spiritual. God I called *immortal Mind*. That which sins, suffers, and dies, I named *mortal mind*. The physical senses, or sensuous nature, I called *error* and *shadow*. Soul I denominated *substance*, because Soul alone is truly substantial. God I characterized as individual entity, but His corporeality I denied. The real I claimed as eternal; and its antipodes, or the temporal, I described as unreal. Spirit I called the *reality;* and matter, the *unreality.*

I knew the human conception of God to be that He was a physically personal being, like unto man; and that the five physical senses are so many witnesses to the physical personality of mind and the real existence of matter; but I learned that these material senses testify falsely, that matter neither sees, hears, nor feels Spirit, and is therefore inadequate to form any proper conception of the infinite Mind. "If I bear witness of myself, my witness is not true." (John v. 31.)

I beheld with ineffable awe our great Master's purpose in not questioning those he healed as to their disease or its symptoms, and his marvellous skill in demanding neither obedience to hygienic laws, nor prescribing drugs to support the divine power which heals. Adoringly I discerned the Principle of his holy heroism and Christian example on the cross, when he refused to drink the "vinegar and gall," a preparation of

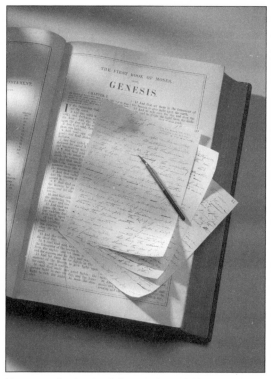

Notes on the book of Genesis, late 1860s. Mary Baker Eddy wrote hundreds of pages of biblical exposition at this time. The pen, belonging to Eddy, is of a later date.

poppy, or aconite, to allay the tortures of crucifixion.

Our great Way-shower, steadfast to the end in his obedience to God's laws, demonstrated for all time and peoples the supremacy of good over evil, and the superiority of Spirit over matter.

The miracles recorded in the Bible, which had before seemed to me supernatural, grew divinely natural and apprehensible; though uninspired interpreters ignorantly pronounce Christ's healing miraculous, instead of seeing therein the operation of the divine law.

Jesus of Nazareth was a natural and divine Scientist. He was so before the material world saw him. He who antedated Abraham, and gave the world a new date in the Christian era, was a Christian Scientist, who needed no discovery of the Science of being in order to rebuke the evidence. To one "born of the flesh," however, divine Science must be a discovery. Woman must give it birth. It must be begotten of spirituality, since none but the pure in heart can see God,— the Principle of all things pure; and none but the "poor in spirit" could first state this Principle, could know yet more of the nothingness of matter and the allness of Spirit, could utilize Truth, and absolutely reduce the demonstration of being, in Science, to the apprehension of the age.

I wrote also, at this period, comments on the Scriptures, setting forth their spiritual interpretation, the Science of the Bible, and so laid the foundation of my work called *Science and Health,* published in 1875.[70]

If these notes and comments, which have never been read by any one but myself, were published, it would show that after my discovery of the absolute Science of Mind-healing, like all great truths, this spiritual Science developed itself to me until *Science and Health* was written. These early comments are valuable to me as waymarks of progress, which I would not have effaced.

Up to that time I had not fully voiced my discovery. Naturally, my first jottings were but efforts to express in feeble diction Truth's ultimate. In Longfellow's language,—

> But the feeble hands and helpless,
> Groping blindly in the darkness,
> Touch God's right hand in that darkness,
> And are lifted up and strengthened.

As sweet music ripples in one's first thoughts of it like the brooklet in its meandering midst pebbles and rocks, before the mind can duly express it to the ear,— so the harmony of divine Science first broke upon my sense, before gathering experience and confidence to articulate it. Its natural manifestation is beautiful and euphonious, but its written expression increases in power and perfection under the guidance of the great Master.

The divine hand led me into a new world of light and Life, a fresh universe — old to God, but new to His "little one." It became evident that the divine Mind alone must answer, and be found as the Life, or Principle, of all being; and that one must acquaint himself with God, if he would be at peace. He must be ours practically, guiding our every thought and action; else we cannot understand the omnipresence of good sufficiently to demonstrate, even in part, the Science of the perfect Mind and divine healing.

I had learned that thought must be spiritualized, in order to apprehend Spirit. It must become honest, unselfish, and pure, in order to have the least understanding of God in divine Science. The first must become last. Our reliance upon material things must be transferred to a perception of and dependence on spiritual things. For Spirit to be supreme in demonstration, it must be supreme in our affections, and we must be clad with divine power. Purity, self-renunciation, faith, and understanding must reduce all things real to their own mental denomination, Mind, which divides, subdivides, increases, diminishes, constitutes, and sustains, according to the law of God.

I had learned that Mind reconstructed the body, and that nothing else could. How it was done, the spiritual Science of Mind must reveal. It was a mystery to me then, but I have since understood it. All Science is a revelation. Its Principle is divine, not human, reaching higher than the stars of heaven.

Am I a believer in spiritualism?[71] I believe in no *ism*. This is my endeavor, to be a Christian, to assimilate the character and practice of the anointed; and no motive can cause a surrender of this effort. As I understand it, spiritualism is the antipode of Christian Science. I esteem all honest people, and love them, and hold to loving our enemies and doing good to them that "despitefully use you and persecute you."

Foundation Work

As the pioneer of Christian Science I stood alone in this conflict, endeavoring to smite error with the falchion of Truth. The rare bequests of Christian Science are costly, and they have won fields of battle from which the dainty borrower would have fled. Ceaseless toil, self-renunciation, and love, have cleared its pathway.

The motive of my earliest labors has never changed. It was to relieve the sufferings of humanity by a sanitary system that should include all moral and religious reform.

It is often asked why Christian Science was revealed to me as one intelligence, analyzing, uncovering, and annihilating the false testimony of the physical senses. Why was this conviction necessary to the right apprehension of the invincible and infinite energies of Truth and Love, as contrasted with the foibles and fables of finite mind and material existence.

The answer is plain. St. Paul declared that the law was the schoolmaster, to bring him to Christ. Even so was I led into the mazes of divine metaphysics through the gospel of suffering, the providence of God, and the cross of Christ. No one else can drain the cup which I have drunk to the dregs as the Discoverer and teacher of Christian Science; neither can its inspiration be gained without tasting this cup.

The loss of material objects of affection sunders the dominant ties of earth and points to heaven. Nothing can compete with Christian Science, and its demonstration, in showing this solemn certainty in growing freedom and vindicating "the ways of God" to man. The absolute proof and self-evident propositions of Truth are immeasurably paramount to rubric and dogma in proving the Christ.

From my very childhood I was impelled, by a hunger and thirst after divine things,— a desire for something higher and better than matter, and apart from it,— to seek diligently for the knowledge of God as the one great and ever-present relief from human woe. The first spontaneous motion of Truth and Love, acting through Christian Science on my roused consciousness, banished at once and forever the fundamental error of faith in things material; for this trust is the unseen sin, the unknown foe,— the heart's untamed desire which breaketh the divine commandments. As says St. James: "Whosoever shall keep the whole law, and yet offend in one point, he is guilty of all."

Into mortal mind's material obliquity I gazed, and stood abashed. Blanched was the cheek of pride. My heart bent low before the omnipotence of Spirit, and a tint of humility, soft as the heart of a moonbeam, mantled the earth. Bethlehem and Bethany, Gethsemane and Calvary, spoke to my chastened sense as by the tearful lips of a babe. Frozen fountains were unsealed. Erudite systems of philosophy and religion melted, for Love unveiled the healing promise and potency of a present spiritual *afflatus*. It was the gospel of healing, on its divinely appointed human mission, bearing on its white wings, to my apprehension, "the beauty of holiness,"— even the possibilities of spiritual insight, knowledge, and being.

Early had I learned that whatever is loved materially, as mere corporeal personality, is eventually lost. "For whosoever will save his life shall lose it," saith the Master. Exultant hope, if tinged with earthliness, is crushed as the moth.

What is termed mortal and material existence is graphically defined by Calderon, the famous Spanish poet, who wrote,—

> What is life? 'T is but a madness.
> What is life? A mere illusion,

Fleeting pleasure, fond delusion,
Short-lived joy, that ends in sadness,
Whose most constant substance seems
But the dream of other dreams.

Medical Experiments

The physical side of this research was aided by hints from homoeopathy, sustaining my final conclusion that mortal belief, instead of the drug, governed the action of material medicine.

I wandered through the dim mazes of *materia medica*, till I was weary of "scientific guessing," as it has been well called. I sought knowledge from the different schools,— allopathy, homoeopathy, hydropathy, electricity, and from various humbugs,— but without receiving satisfaction.[72]

I found, in the two hundred and sixty-two remedies enumerated by Jahr,[73] one pervading secret; namely, that the less material medicine we have, and the more Mind, the better the work is done; a fact which seems to prove the Principle of Mind-healing. One drop of the thirtieth attenuation of *Natrum muriaticum*,[74] in a tumbler-full of water, and one teaspoonful of the water mixed with the faith of ages, would cure patients not affected by a larger dose. The drug disappears in the higher attenuations of homoeopathy, and matter is thereby rarefied to its fatal essence, mortal mind; but immortal Mind, the curative Principle, remains, and is found to be even more active.

The mental virtues of the material methods of medicine, when understood, were insufficient to satisfy my doubts as to the honesty or utility of using a material curative. I must know more of the unmixed,

Dr. William T. Vail's Hydropathic Institute, Hill, New Hampshire. Mary Baker Eddy spent about three months here in 1862, taking the "water cure."

unerring source, in order to gain the Science of Mind, the All-in-all of Spirit, in which matter is obsolete. Nothing less could solve the mental problem. If I sought an answer from the medical schools, the reply was dark and contradictory. Neither ancient nor modern philosophy could clear the clouds, or give me one distinct statement of the spiritual Science of Mind-healing. Human reason was not equal to it.

I claim for healing scientifically the following advantages: *First:* It does away with all material medicines, and recognizes the antidote for all sickness, as well as sin, in the immortal Mind; and mortal mind as the source of all the ills which befall mortals. *Second:* It is more effectual than drugs, and cures when they fail, or only relieve; thus proving the superiority of metaphysics over physics. *Third:* A person healed by Christian Science is not only healed of his disease, but he is advanced morally and spiritually. The mortal body being but the objective state of the mortal mind, this mind must be renovated to improve the body.

First Publication

In 1870 I copyrighted the first publication on spiritual, scientific Mind-healing, entitled *The Science of Man.* This little book is converted into the chapter on "Recapitulation" in *Science and Health.* It was so new— the basis it laid down for physical and moral health was so hopelessly original, and men were so unfamiliar with the subject— that I did not venture upon its publication until later, having learned that the merits of Christian Science must be proven before a work on this subject could be profitably published.

The truths of Christian Science are not interpolations of the Scriptures, but the spiritual interpretations thereof. Science is the prism of Truth, which divides its rays and brings out the hues of Deity. Human hypotheses have darkened the glow and grandeur of evangelical religion. When speaking of his true followers in every period, Jesus said, "*They* shall lay hands on the sick, and they shall recover." There is no authority for querying the authenticity of this declaration, for it already was and is demonstrated as practical, and its claim is substantiated,— a claim too immanent to fall to the ground beneath the stroke of artless workmen.

Though a man were girt with the Urim and Thummim of priestly office, and denied the perpetuity of Jesus' command, "Heal the sick," or its application in all time to those who understand Christ as the Truth and the Life, that man would not expound the gospel according to Jesus.

Five years after taking out my first copyright, I taught the Science of Mind-healing, *alias* Christian Science, by writing out my manuscripts for students and distributing them unsparingly. This will account for certain published and unpublished manuscripts extant, which the evil-minded would insinuate did not originate with me.

The Precious Volume

The first edition of my most important work, *Science and Health,* containing the complete statement of Christian Science,— the term employed by me to express the divine, or spiritual, Science of Mind-healing, was published in 1875.

When it was first printed, the critics took pleasure in saying, "This book is indeed wholly original, but it will never be read."

The first edition numbered one thousand copies. In September, 1891, it had reached sixty-two editions.

Those who formerly sneered at it, as foolish and eccentric, now declare Bishop Berkeley, David Hume, Ralph Waldo Emerson, or certain German philosophers, to have been the originators of the Science of Mind-healing as therein stated.

Even the Scriptures gave no direct interpretation of the scientific basis for demonstrating the spiritual Principle of healing, until our heavenly Father saw fit, through the Key to the Scriptures, in *Science and Health,* to unlock this "mystery of godliness."

Printer's bill, dated October 30, 1875, for the publication of one thousand copies of the first edition of *Science and Health*.

My reluctance to give the public, in my first edition of *Science and Health*, the chapter on "Animal Magnetism,"[75] and the divine purpose that this should be done, may have an interest for the reader, and will be seen in the following circumstances. I had finished that edition as far as that chapter, when the printer informed me that he could not go on with my work. I had already paid him seven hundred dollars, and yet he stopped my work. All efforts to persuade him to finish my book were in vain.

After months had passed, I yielded to a constant conviction that I must insert in my last chapter a partial history of what I had already observed of mental malpractice. Accordingly, I set to work, contrary to

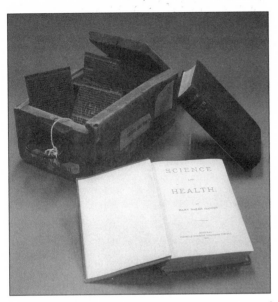

A first edition of *Science and Health* (1875), with some of the original plates used in printing the book.

my inclination, to fulfil this painful task, and finished my copy for the book. As it afterwards appeared, although I had not thought of such a result, my printer resumed his work at the same time, finished printing the copy he had on hand, and then started for Lynn to see me. The afternoon that he left Boston for Lynn, I started for Boston with my finished copy. We met at the Eastern depot in Lynn, and were both surprised,— I to learn that he had printed all the copy on hand, and had come to tell me he wanted more,— he to find me *en route* for Boston, to give him the closing chapter of my first edition of *Science and Health*. Not a word had passed between us, audibly or mentally, while this went on. I had grown disgusted with my printer, and become silent. He had come to a standstill through motives and circumstances unknown to me.

Science and Health is the textbook of Christian Science. Whosoever learns the letter of this book, must also gain its spiritual significance, in order to demonstrate Christian Science.

When the demand for this book increased, and people were healed simply by reading it, the copyright was infringed. I entered a suit at law, and my copyright was protected.[76]

Recuperative Incident

Through four successive years I healed, preached, and taught in a general way, refusing to take any pay for my services and living on a small annuity.

At one time I was called to speak before the Lyceum Club, at Westerly, Rhode Island. On my arrival my hostess told me that her next-door neighbor was dying. I asked permission to see her. It was granted, and with my hostess I went to the invalid's house.

The physicians had given up the case and retired. I had stood by her side about fifteen minutes when the sick woman rose from her bed, dressed herself, and was well. Afterwards they showed me the clothes already prepared for her burial; and told me that her physicians had said the diseased condition was caused by an injury received from a surgical operation at the birth of her last babe, and that it was impossible for her to be delivered of another child. It is sufficient to add her babe was safely born, and weighed twelve pounds. The mother afterwards wrote to me, "I never before suffered so little in childbirth."

This scientific demonstration so stirred the doctors and clergy that they had my notices for a second lecture pulled down, and refused me a hearing in their halls and churches. This circumstance is cited simply to show the opposition which Christian Science encountered a quarter-century ago, as contrasted with its present welcome into the sickroom.

Many were the desperate cases I instantly healed, "without money and without price," and in most instances without even an acknowledgment of the benefit.

A True Man

My last marriage was with Asa Gilbert Eddy,[77] and was a blessed and spiritual union, solemnized at Lynn, Massachusetts, by the Rev. Samuel Barrett Stewart, in the year 1877. Dr. Eddy was the first student publicly to announce himself a Christian Scientist, and place these symbolic words on his office sign. He forsook all to follow in this line of light. He was the first organizer of a Christian Science Sunday School, which he superintended. He also taught a special Bible-class; and he lectured so ably on Scriptural topics that clergymen of other denominations listened

to him with deep interest. He was remarkably successful in Mind-healing, and untiring in his chosen work. In 1882 he passed away, with a smile of peace and love resting on his serene countenance. "Mark the perfect *man*, and behold the upright: for the end of *that* man *is* peace. (Psalms xxxvii. 37.)

Asa Gilbert Eddy. This ambrotype of Mary Baker Eddy's third husband predates by more than a decade their marriage, which took place in 1877.

College and Church

In 1867 I introduced the first purely metaphysical system of healing since the apostolic days. I began by teaching one student Christian Science Mind-healing. From this seed grew the Massachusetts Metaphysical College in Boston, chartered in 1881. No charter was granted for similar purposes after 1883. It is the only College, hitherto, for teaching the pathology of spiritual power, *alias* the Science of Mind-healing.

My husband, Asa G. Eddy, taught two terms in my College. After I gave up teaching, my adopted son, Ebenezer J. Foster Eddy,[78] a graduate of the Hahnemann Medical College of Philadelphia, and who also received a certificate from Dr. W. W. Keen's (allopathic) Philadelphia School of Anatomy and Surgery,—having renounced his material method of practice and embraced the teachings of Christian Science, taught the Primary, Normal, and Obstetric class one term. Gen. Erastus N. Bates taught one Primary class, in 1889, after which I judged it best to close the institution. These students of mine were the only assistant teachers in the College.

The first Christian Scientist Association was organized by myself and six of my students in 1876, on the Centennial Day of our nation's freedom. At a meeting of the Christian Scientist Association, on April 12, 1879, it was voted to organize a church to commemorate the words and works of our Master, a Mind-healing church, without a creed, to be called the Church of Christ, Scientist, the first such church ever organized. The charter for this church was obtained in June, 1879, and during the same month the members, twenty-six in number, extended a call to me to become their pastor. I accepted the call, and was ordained in 1881, though I had preached five years before being ordained.

The house in Lynn at 8, later 12, Broad Street. Mary Baker Eddy owned this photograph, and she identified the man visible in the second-floor window as her husband, Asa Gilbert Eddy.

When I was its pastor, and in the pulpit every Sunday, my church increased in members, and its spiritual growth kept pace with its increasing popularity; but when obliged, because of accumulating work in the College, to preach only occasionally, no student, at that time, was found able to maintain the church in its previous harmony and prosperity.

Examining the situation prayerfully and carefully, noting the church's need, and the predisposing and exciting cause of its condition, I saw that the crisis had come when much time and attention must be given to defend this church from the envy and molestation of other churches, and from the danger to its members which must always lie in Christian warfare. At this juncture I recommended that the church be dissolved. No sooner were my views made known, than the proper measures were adopted to carry them out, the votes passing without a dissenting voice.

This measure was immediately followed by a great revival of mutual love, prosperity, and spiritual power.

The history of that hour holds this true record. Adding to its ranks and influence, this spiritually organized Church of Christ, Scientist, in Boston, still goes on. A new light broke in upon it, and more beautiful became the garments of her who "bringeth good tidings, that publisheth peace."

Despite the prosperity of my church, it was learned that material organization has its value and peril, and that organization is requisite only in the earliest periods in Christian history. After this material form of cohesion and fellowship has accomplished its end, continued organization retards spiritual growth, and should be laid off,— even as the corporeal organization deemed requisite in the first stages of mortal existence is finally laid off, in order to gain spiritual freedom and supremacy.

From careful observation and experience came my clue to the uses and abuses of organization. Therefore, in accord with my special request, followed that noble, unprecedented action of the Christian Scientist Association connected with my College when dissolving that organization,— in forgiving enemies, returning good for evil, in following Jesus' command, "Whosoever shall smite thee on thy right cheek, turn to him the other also." I saw these fruits of Spirit, long-suffering and temperance, fulfil the law of Christ in righteousness. I also saw that Christianity has withstood less the temptation of popularity than of persecution.

"Feed My Sheep"

Lines penned when I was pastor of the Church of Christ, Scientist, in Boston.

Shepherd, show me how to go
    O'er the hillside steep,
How to gather, how to sow,—
    How to feed Thy sheep;
I will listen for Thy voice,
    Lest my footsteps stray;
I will follow and rejoice
    All the rugged way.

Thou wilt bind the stubborn will,
    Wound the callous breast,
Make self-righteousness be still,
    Break earth's stupid rest.
Strangers on a barren shore,
    Lab'ring long and lone,
We would enter by the door,
    And Thou know'st Thine own.

So, when day grows dark and cold,
    Tear or triumph harms,
Lead Thy lambkins to the fold,
    Take them in Thine arms;
Feed the hungry, heal the heart,
    Till the morning's beam;
White as wool, ere they depart,
    Shepherd, wash them clean.

College Closed

The apprehension of what has been, and must be, the final outcome of material organization, which wars with Love's spiritual compact, caused me to dread the unprecedented popularity of my College. Students from all over our continent, and from Europe, were flooding the school. At this time there were over three hundred applications from persons desiring to enter the College, and applicants were rapidly increasing. Example had shown the dangers arising from being placed on earthly pinnacles, and Christian Science shuns whatever involves material means for the promotion of spiritual ends.

In view of all this, a meeting was called of the Board of Directors of my College, who, being informed of my intentions, unanimously voted that the school be discontinued.

A Primary class student, richly imbued with the spirit of Christ, is a better healer and teacher than a Normal class

569 and 571 Columbus Avenue, Boston. These gray stone buildings were the site of the Massachusetts Metaphysical College, 1882–1889.

student who partakes less of God's love. After having received instructions in a Primary class from me, or a loyal student, and afterwards studied thoroughly *Science and Health,* a student can enter upon the gospel work of teaching Christian Science, and so fulfil the command of Christ. But before entering this field of labor he must have studied the latest editions of my works, be a good Bible scholar and a consecrated Christian.

The Massachusetts Metaphysical College drew its breath from me, but I was yearning for retirement. The question was, Who else could sustain this institute, under all that was aimed at its vital purpose, the establishment of *genuine* Christian Science healing? My conscientious scruples about diplomas, the recent experience of the church fresh in my thoughts, and the growing conviction that every one should build on his own foundation, subject to the one builder and maker, God,— all these considerations moved me to close my flourishing school, and the following resolutions were passed:—

At a special meeting of the Board of the Metaphysical College Corporation, Oct. 29, 1889, the following are some of the resolutions which were presented and passed unanimously:—

WHEREAS, The Massachusetts Metaphysical College, chartered in January, 1881, for medical purposes, to give instruction in scientific methods of mental healing on a purely practical basis, to impart a thorough understanding of metaphysics, to restore health, hope, and harmony to man,—has fulfilled its high and noble destiny, and sent to all parts of our country, and into foreign lands, students instructed in Christian Science Mind-healing, to meet the demand of the age for something higher than physic or drugging; and

WHEREAS, The material organization was, in the beginning in this institution, like the baptism of Jesus, of which he said, "Suffer it to be so now," though the teaching was a purely spiritual and scientific impartation of Truth, whose Christly spirit has led to higher ways, means, and understanding,—the President, the Rev. Mary B. G. Eddy, at the height of prosperity in the institution, which yields a large income, is willing to sacrifice all for the advancement of the world in Truth and Love; and

WHEREAS, Other institutions for instruction in Christian Science, which are working out their periods of organization, will doubtless follow the example of the *Alma Mater* after having accomplished the worthy purpose for which they were organized, and the hour has come wherein the great need is for more of the spirit instead of the letter, and *Science and Health* is adapted to work this result; and

WHEREAS, The fundamental principle for growth in Christian Science is spiritual formation first, last, and always, while in human growth material organization is first; and

WHEREAS, Mortals must learn to lose their estimate of the powers that are not ordained of God, and attain the bliss of loving unselfishly, working patiently, and conquering all that is unlike Christ and the example he gave; therefore

Resolved, That we thank the State for its charter, which is the only one ever granted to a *legal college* for teaching the Science of Mind-healing; that we thank the public for its liberal patronage. And everlasting gratitude is due to the President, for her great and noble work, which we believe will prove a healing for the nations, and bring all men to a knowledge of the true God, uniting them in one common brotherhood.

> After due deliberation and earnest discussion it was unanimously
> voted: That as all debts of the corporation have been paid, it is deemed
> best to dissolve this corporation, and the same is hereby dissolved.
>
> C. A. Frye, Clerk[79]

When God impelled me to set a price on my instruction in Christian Science Mind-healing, I could think of no financial equivalent for an impartation of a knowledge of that divine power which heals; but I was led to name three hundred dollars as the price for each pupil in one course of lessons at my College,— a startling sum for tuition lasting barely three weeks. This amount greatly troubled me. I shrank from asking it, but was finally led, by a strange providence, to accept this fee.

God has since shown me, in multitudinous ways, the wisdom of this decision; and I beg disinterested people to ask my loyal students if they consider three hundred dollars any real equivalent for my instruction during twelve half-days, or even in half as many lessons. Nevertheless, my list of indigent charity scholars is very large, and I have had as many as seventeen in one class.

Loyal students speak with delight of their pupilage, and of what it has done for them, and for others through them. By loyalty in students I mean this,— allegiance to God, subordination of the human to the divine, steadfast justice, and strict adherence to divine Truth and Love.

I see clearly that students in Christian Science should, at present, continue to organize churches, schools, and associations for the furtherance and unfolding of Truth, and that my necessity is not necessarily theirs; but it was the Father's opportunity for furnishing a new rule of order in divine Science, and the blessings which arose therefrom. Students are not environed with such obstacles as were encountered in the beginning of pioneer work.

In December, 1889, I gave a lot of land in Boston to my student, Mr. Ira O. Knapp of Roslindale,— valued in 1892 at about twenty thousand dollars, and rising in value,— to be appropriated for the erection, and building on the premises thereby conveyed, of a church edifice to be used as a temple for Christian Science worship.

General Associations, and Our Magazine

For many successive years I have endeavored to find new ways and means for the promotion and expansion of scientific Mind-healing, seeking to broaden its channels and, if possible, to build a hedge round about it that should shelter its perfections from the contaminating influences of those who have a small portion of its letter and less of its spirit. At the same time I have worked to provide a home for every true seeker and honest worker in this vineyard of Truth.

To meet the broader wants of humanity, and provide folds for the sheep that were without shepherds, I suggested to my

The first issue of the *Journal of Christian Science*, April 14, 1883. Renamed *The Christian Science Journal* in 1885, this publication was edited by Mary Baker Eddy for several years.

students, in 1886, the propriety of forming a National Christian Scientist Association. This was immediately done, and delegations from the Christian Scientist Association of the Massachusetts Metaphysical College, and from branch associations in other States, met in general convention at New York City, February 11, 1886.

The first official organ of the Christian Scientist Association was called *Journal of Christian Science.* I started it, April, 1883, as editor and publisher.

To the National Christian Scientist Association, at its meeting in Cleveland, Ohio, June, 1889, I sent a letter, presenting to its loyal members *The Christian Science Journal,* as it was now called, and the funds belonging thereto. This monthly magazine had been made successful and prosperous under difficult circumstances, and was designed to bear aloft the standard of genuine Christian Science.

Faith-cure

It is often asked, Why are faith-cures sometimes more speedy than some of the cures wrought through Christian Scientists? Because faith is belief, and not understanding; and it is easier to believe, than to understand spiritual Truth. It demands less cross-bearing, self-renunciation, and divine Science to admit the claims of the corporeal senses and appeal to God for relief through a humanized conception of His power, than to deny these claims and learn the divine way,— drinking Jesus' cup, being baptized with his baptism, gaining the end through persecution and purity.

Millions are believing in God, or good, without bearing the fruits of goodness, not having reached its Science. Belief is virtually blindness, when it admits Truth without understanding it. Blind belief cannot say with the apostle, "I know whom I have believed." There is danger in this mental state called belief; for if Truth is admitted, but not understood, it may be lost, and error may enter through this same channel of ignorant belief. The faith-cure has devout followers, whose Christian practice is far in advance of their theory.

The work of healing, in the Science of Mind, is the most sacred and salutary power which can be wielded. My Christian students, impressed with the true sense of the great work before them, enter this strait and narrow path, and work conscientiously.

Let us follow the example of Jesus, the master Metaphysician, and gain sufficient knowledge of error to destroy it with Truth. Evil is not mastered by evil; it can only be overcome with good. This brings out the nothingness of evil and the eternal somethingness, vindicates the divine Principle, and improves the race of Adam.

Foundation-stones

The following ideas of Deity, antagonized by finite theories, doctrines, and hypotheses, I found to be demonstrable rules in Christian Science, and that we must abide by them.

Whatever diverges from the one divine Mind, or God,— or divides Mind into minds, Spirit into spirits, Soul into souls, and Being into beings,— is a misstatement of the unerring divine Principle of Science, which interrupts the meaning of the omnipotence, omniscience, and omnipresence of Spirit, and is of human instead of divine origin.

War is waged between the evidences of Spirit and the evidences of the five physical senses; and this contest must go on until peace be declared by the final triumph of Spirit in immutable harmony. Divine Science disclaims sin, sickness, and death, on the basis of the omnipotence and omnipresence of God, or divine good.

All consciousness is Mind, and Mind is God. Hence there is but one Mind; and that one is the infinite good, supplying all Mind by the reflection, not the subdivision, of God. Whatever else claims to be mind, or consciousness, is untrue. The sun sends forth light, but not suns; so God reflects Himself, or Mind, but does not subdivide Mind, or good, into minds, good and evil. Divine Science demands mighty wrestlings with mortal beliefs, as we sail into the eternal haven over the unfathomable sea of possibilities.

Neither ancient nor modern philosophy furnishes a scientific basis for the Science of Mind-healing. Plato believed he had a soul, which must be doctored in order to heal his body. This would be like correcting the principle of music for the purpose of destroying discord. Principle is right; it is practice that is wrong. Soul is right; it is the flesh that is evil. Soul is the synonym of Spirit, God; hence there is but one Soul, and that one is infinite. If that pagan philosopher had known that physical sense, not Soul, causes all bodily ailments, his philosophy would have yielded to Science.

Man shines by borrowed light. He reflects God as his Mind, and this reflection is substance,— the substance of good. Matter is substance in error, Spirit is substance in Truth.

Evil, or error, is not Mind; but infinite Mind is sufficient to supply all manifestations of intelligence. The notion of more than one Mind, or Life, is as unsatisfying as it is unscientific. All must be of God, and not our own, separated from Him.

Human systems of philosophy and religion are departures from

Christian Science. Mistaking divine Principle for corporeal personality, ingrafting upon one First Cause such opposite effects as good and evil, health and sickness, life and death; making mortality the status and rule of divinity,— such methods can never reach the perfection and demonstration of metaphysical, or Christian Science.

Stating the divine Principle, omnipotence *(omnis potens),* and then departing from this statement and taking the rule of finite matter, with which to work out the problem of infinity or Spirit,— all this is like trying to compensate for the absence of omnipotence by a physical, false, and finite substitute.

With our Master, life was not merely a sense of existence, but an accompanying sense of power that subdued matter and brought to light immortality, insomuch that the people "were astonished at his doctrine: for he taught them as one having authority, and not as the scribes." Life, as defined by Jesus, had no beginning; it was not the result of organization, or infused into matter; it was Spirit.

The Great Revelation

Christian Science reveals the grand verity, that to believe man has a finite and erring mind, and consequently a mortal mind and soul and life, is error. Scientific terms have no contradictory significations.

In Science, Life is not temporal, but eternal, without beginning or ending. The word *Life* never means that which is the source of death, and of good and evil. Such an inference is unscientific. It is like saying that addition means subtraction in one instance and addition in another, and then applying this rule to a demonstration of the science of numbers;

even as mortals apply finite terms to God, in demonstration of infinity. *Life* is a term used to indicate Deity; and every other name for the Supreme Being, if properly employed, has the signification of Life. Whatever errs is mortal, and is the antipodes of Life, or God, and of health and holiness, both in idea and demonstration.

Christian Science reveals Mind, the only living and true God, and all that is made by Him, Mind, as harmonious, immortal, and spiritual: the five material senses define Mind and matter as distinct, but mutually dependent, each on the other, for intelligence and existence. Science defines man as immortal, as coexistent and coeternal with God, as made in His own image and likeness; material sense defines life as something apart from God, beginning and ending, and man as very far from the divine likeness. Science reveals Life as a complete sphere, as eternal, self-existent Mind; material sense defines life as a broken sphere, as organized matter, and mind as something separate from God. Science reveals Spirit as All, averring that there is nothing beside God; material sense says that matter, His antipode, is something besides God. Material sense adds that the divine Spirit created matter, and that matter and evil are as real as Spirit and good.

Christian Science reveals God and His idea as the All and Only. It declares that evil is the absence of good; whereas, good is God ever-present, and therefore evil is unreal and good is all that is real. Christian Science saith to the wave and storm, "Be still," and there is a great calm. Material sense asks, in its ignorance of Science, "When will the raging of the material elements cease?" Science saith to all manner of disease, "Know that God is all-power and all-presence, and there is nothing beside Him;" and the sick are healed. Material sense saith, "Oh, when will my sufferings cease? Where is God? Sickness is something besides Him, which He cannot, or does not, heal."

Christian Science is the only sure basis of harmony. Material sense contradicts Science, for matter and its so-called organizations take no cognizance of the spiritual facts of the universe, or of the real man and God. Christian Science declares that there is but one Truth, Life, Love, but one Spirit, Mind, Soul. Any attempt to divide these arises from the fallibility of sense, from mortal man's ignorance, from enmity to God and divine Science.

Christian Science declares that sickness is a belief, a latent fear, made manifest on the body in different forms of fear or disease. This fear is formed unconsciously in the silent thought, as when you awaken from sleep and feel ill, experiencing the effect of a fear whose existence you do not realize; but if you fall asleep, actually conscious of the truth of Christian Science,— namely, that man's harmony is no more to be invaded than the rhythm of the universe,— you cannot awake in fear or suffering of any sort.

Science saith to fear, "You are the cause of all sickness; but you are a self-constituted falsity,— you are darkness, nothingness. You are without 'hope, and without God in the world.' You do not exist, and have no right to exist, for 'perfect Love casteth out fear.'"

God is everywhere. "There is no speech nor language, where their voice is not heard;" and this voice is Truth that destroys error and Love that casts out fear.

Christian Science reveals the fact that, if suffering exists, it is in the mortal mind only, for matter has no sensation and cannot suffer.

If you rule out every sense of disease and suffering from mortal mind, it cannot be found in the body.

Posterity will have the right to demand that Christian Science be stated and demonstrated in its godliness and grandeur,— that however little be taught or learned, that little shall be right. Let there be milk for babes, but let not the milk be adulterated. Unless this method be pursued, the Science of Christian healing will again be lost, and human suffering will increase.

Test Christian Science by its effect on society, and you will find that the views here set forth — as to the illusion of sin, sickness, and death — bring forth better fruits of health, righteousness, and Life, than *a belief in their reality has ever done*. A demonstration of the *unreality* of evil destroys evil.

Sin, Sinner, and Ecclesiasticism

Why do Christian Scientists say God and His idea are the only realities, and then insist on the need of healing sickness and sin? Because Christian Science heals sin as it heals sickness, by establishing the recognition that God *is All*, and there is none beside Him, — that all is good, and there is in reality no evil, neither sickness nor sin. We attack the sinner's belief in the pleasure of sin, *alias* the reality of sin, which makes him a sinner, in order to destroy this belief and save him from sin; and we attack the belief of the sick in the reality of sickness, in order to heal them. When we deny the authority of sin, we begin to sap it; for this denunciation must precede its destruction.

God is good, hence goodness is something, for it represents God, the Life of man. Its opposite, nothing, named *evil*, is nothing but a conspiracy against man's Life and goodness. Do you not feel bound to expose this conspiracy, and so to save man from it? Whosoever covers iniquity becomes accessory to it. Sin, as a claim, is more dangerous than sickness, more subtle, more difficult to heal.

St. Augustine once said, "The devil is but the ape of God." Sin is worse than sickness; but recollect that it encourages sin to say, "There is no sin," and leave the subject there.

Sin ultimates in sinner, and in this sense they are one. You cannot separate sin from the sinner, nor the sinner from his sin. The sin is the sinner, and *vice versa,* for such is the unity of evil; and together both sinner and sin will be destroyed by the supremacy of good. This, however, does not annihilate man, for to efface sin, *alias* the sinner, brings to light, makes apparent, the real man, even God's "image and likeness." Need it be said that any opposite theory is heterodox to divine Science, which teaches that good is equally *one* and *all,* even as the opposite claim of evil is one.

In Christian Science the fact is made obvious that the sinner and the sin are alike simply nothingness; and this view is supported by the Scripture, where the Psalmist saith: "He shall go to the generation of his fathers; they shall never see light. Man that is in honor, and understandeth not, is like the beasts that perish." God's ways and works and thoughts have never changed, either in Principle or practice.

Since there is in belief an illusion termed sin, which must be met and mastered, we classify sin, sickness, and death as illusions. They are supposititious claims of error; and error being a false claim, they are no claims at all. It is scientific to abide in conscious harmony, in health-giving, deathless Truth and Love. To do this, mortals must first open their eyes to all the illusive forms, methods, and subtlety of error, in order that the illusion, error, may be destroyed; if this is not done, mortals will become the victims of error.

If evangelical churches refuse fellowship with the Church of Christ, Scientist, or with Christian Science, they must rest their opinions of Truth and Love on the evidences of the physical senses, rather than on the teaching and practice of Jesus, or the works of the Spirit.

Ritualism and dogma lead to self-righteousness and bigotry, which freeze out the spiritual element. Pharisaism killeth; Spirit giveth Life. The odors of persecution, tobacco, and alcohol are not the sweet-smelling savor of Truth and Love. Feasting the senses, gratification of appetite and passion, have no warrant in the gospel or the Decalogue. Mortals must take up the cross if they would follow Christ, and worship the Father "in spirit and in truth."

The Jewish religion was not spiritual; hence Jesus denounced it.[80] If the religion of to-day is constituted of such elements as of old ruled Christ out of the synagogues, it will continue to avoid whatever follows the example of our Lord and prefers Christ to creed. Christian Science is the pure evangelic truth. It accords with the trend and tenor of Christ's teaching and example, while it demonstrates the power of Christ as taught in the four Gospels. Truth, casting out evils and healing the sick; Love, fulfilling the law and keeping man unspotted from the world,—these practical manifestations of Christianity constitute the only evangelism, and they need no creed.

As well expect to determine, without a telescope, the magnitude and distance of the stars, as to expect to obtain health, harmony, and holiness through an unspiritual and unhealing religion. Christianity reveals God as ever-present Truth and Love, to be utilized in healing the sick, in casting out error, in raising the dead.

Christian Science gives vitality to religion, which is no longer buried in materiality. It raises men from a material sense into the spiritual understanding and scientific demonstration of God.

The Human Concept

Sin existed as a false claim before the human concept of sin was formed; hence one's concept of error is not the whole of error. The human thought does not constitute sin, but *vice versa,* sin constitutes the human or physical concept.

Sin is both concrete and abstract. Sin was, and is, the lying supposition that life, substance, and intelligence are both material and spiritual, and yet are separate from God. The first iniquitous manifestation of sin was a finity. The finite was self-arrayed against the infinite, the mortal against immortality, and a sinner was the antipode of God.

Silencing self, *alias* rising above corporeal personality, is what reforms the sinner and destroys sin. In the ratio that the testimony of material personal sense ceases, sin diminishes, until the false claim called sin is finally lost for lack of witness.

The sinner created neither himself nor sin, but sin created the sinner; that is, error made its man mortal, and this mortal was the image and likeness of evil, not of good. Therefore the lie was, and *is,* collective as well as individual. It was in no way contingent on Adam's thought, but supposititiously self-created. In the words of our Master, it, the "devil" (*alias* evil), "was a liar, and the father of it."

This mortal material concept was never a creator, although as a serpent it claimed to originate in the name of "the Lord," or good,—original evil; second, in the name of human concept, it claimed to beget the offspring of evil, *alias* an evil offspring. However, the human concept never was, neither indeed can be, the father of man. Even the spiritual idea, or ideal man, is not a parent, though he reflects the infinity of good. The great difference between these opposites is, that the human material concept is *unreal,* and the divine concept or idea is spiritually real. One is false, while the other is true. One is temporal, but the other is eternal.

Our Master instructed his students to "call no man your father upon the earth: for one is your Father, which is in heaven." (Matt. xxiii. 9.)

Science and Health, the textbook of Christian Science, treats of the human concept, and the transference of thought, as follows:—

"How can matter originate or transmit mind? We answer that it cannot. Darkness and doubt encompass thought, so long as it bases creation on materiality" (p. 551).

"In reality there is no *mortal* mind, and consequently no transference of mortal thought and will-power. Life and being are of God. In Christian Science, man can do no harm, for scientific thoughts are true thoughts, passing from God to man" (pp. 103, 104).

"Man is the offspring of Spirit. The beautiful, good, and pure constitute his ancestry. His origin is not, like that of mortals, in brute instinct, nor does he pass through material conditions prior to reaching intelligence. Spirit is his primitive and ultimate source of being; God is his Father, and Life is the law of his being" (p. 63).

"The parent of all human discord was the Adam-dream, the deep sleep, in which originated the delusion that life and intelligence proceeded from and passed into matter. This pantheistic error, or so-called *serpent,* insists still upon the opposite of Truth, saying, 'Ye shall be as gods;' that is, I will make error as real and eternal as Truth. . . . 'I will put spirit into what I call matter, and matter shall seem to have life as much as God, Spirit, who *is* the only Life.' This error has proved itself to be error. Its life is found to be not Life, but only a transient, false sense of an existence which ends in death" (pp. 306, 307).

"When will the error of believing that there is life in matter, and that sin, sickness, and death are creations of God, be unmasked? When will it be understood that matter has no intelligence, life, nor sensation, and that the opposite belief is the prolific source of all suffering? God created all through Mind, and made all perfect and eternal. Where then is the necessity for recreation or procreation?" (p. 205).

"Above error's awful din, blackness, and chaos, the voice of Truth still calls: 'Adam, where art thou? Consciousness, where art thou? Art thou dwelling in the belief that mind is in matter, and that evil is mind, or art thou in the living faith that there is and can be but one God, and keeping His commandment?'" (pp. 307, 308).

"Mortal mind inverts the true likeness, and confers animal names and natures upon its own misconceptions. Ignorant of the origin and operations of mortal mind, — that is, ignorant of itself, — this so-called mind puts forth its own qualities, and claims God as their author; . . . usurps the deific prerogatives and is an attempted infringement on infinity" (pp. 512, 513).

We do not question the authenticity of the Scriptural narrative of the Virgin-mother and Bethlehem babe, and the Messianic mission of Christ Jesus; but in our time no Christian Scientist will give chimerical wings to his imagination, or advance speculative theories as to the recurrence of such events.

No person can take the individual place of the Virgin Mary. No person can compass or fulfil the individual mission of Jesus of Nazareth. No person can take the place of the author of *Science and Health,* the Discoverer and Founder of Christian Science. Each individual must fill his own niche in time and eternity.

The second appearing of Jesus is, unquestionably, the spiritual advent of the advancing idea of God, as in Christian Science.

And the scientific ultimate of this God-idea must be, will be, forever individual, incorporeal, and infinite, even the reflection, "image and likeness," of the infinite God.

The right teacher of Christian Science lives the truth he teaches. Preeminent among men, he virtually stands at the head of all sanitary, civil, moral, and religious reform. Such a post of duty, unpierced by vanity, exalts a mortal beyond human praise, or monuments which weigh dust, and humbles him with the tax it raises on calamity to open the gates of heaven. It is not the forager on others' wisdom that God thus crowns, but he who is obedient to the divine command, "Render to Caesar the things that are Caesar's, and to God the things that are God's."

Great temptations beset an ignorant or an unprincipled mind-practice in opposition to the straight and narrow path of Christian Science. Promiscuous mental treatment, without the consent or knowledge of the individual treated, is an error of much magnitude. People unaware of the indications of mental treatment, know not what is affecting them, and thus may be robbed of their individual rights,— freedom of choice and self-government. Who is willing to be subjected to such an influence? Ask the unbridled mind-manipulator if he would consent to this; and if not, then he is knowingly transgressing Christ's command. He who secretly manipulates mind without the permission of man or God, is not dealing justly and loving mercy, according to pure and undefiled religion.

Sinister and selfish motives entering into mental practice are dangerous incentives; they proceed from false convictions and a fatal ignorance. These are the tares growing side by side with the wheat, that must be recognized, and uprooted, before the wheat can be garnered and Christian Science demonstrated.

Secret mental efforts to obtain help from one who is unaware of this attempt, demoralizes the person who does this, the same as other forms of stealing, and will end in destroying health and morals.

In the practice of Christian Science one cannot impart a mental influence that hazards another's happiness, nor interfere with the rights of the individual. To disregard the welfare of others is contrary to the law of God; therefore it deteriorates one's ability to do good, to benefit himself and mankind.

The Psalmist vividly portrays the result of secret faults, presumptuous sins, and self-deception, in these words: "How are they brought into desolation, as in a moment! They are utterly consumed with terrors."

Personality

The immortal man being spiritual, individual, and eternal, his mortal opposite must be material, corporeal, and temporal. Physical personality is finite; but God is infinite. He is without materiality, without finiteness of form or Mind.

Limitations are put off in proportion as the fleshly nature disappears and man is found in the reflection of Spirit.

This great fact leads into profound depths. The material human concept grew beautifully less as I floated into more spiritual latitudes and purer realms of thought.

From that hour personal corporeality became less to me than it is to people who fail to appreciate individual character. I endeavored to lift thought above physical personality, or selfhood in matter, to man's spiritual individuality in God,— in the true Mind, where sensible evil is lost in supersensible good. This is the only way whereby the false personality is laid off.

He who clings to personality, or perpetually warns you of "personality," wrongs it, or terrifies people over it, and is the sure victim of his own corporeality. Constantly to scrutinize physical personality, or accuse people of being unduly personal, is like the sick talking sickness. Such errancy betrays a violent and egotistical personality, increases one's sense of corporeality, and begets a fear of the senses and a perpetually egotistical sensibility.

He who does this is ignorant of the meaning of the word *personality,* and defines it by his own *corpus sine pectore* (soulless body), and fails to distinguish the individual, or real man from the false sense of corporeality, or egotistic self.

My own corporeal personality afflicteth me not wittingly; for I desire never to think of it, and it cannot think of me.

Plagiarism

The various forms of book-borrowing without credit[81] spring from this ill-concealed question in mortal mind, Who shall be greatest? This error violates the law given by Moses, it tramples upon Jesus' Sermon on the Mount, it does violence to the ethics of Christian Science.

Why withhold my name, while appropriating my language and ideas, but give credit when citing from the works of other authors?

Life and its ideals are inseparable, and one's writings on ethics, and demonstration of Truth, are not, cannot be, understood or taught by those who persistently misunderstand or misrepresent the author. Jesus said, "For there is no man which shall do a miracle in my name, that can lightly speak evil of me."

If one's spiritual ideal is comprehended and loved, the borrower from it is embraced in the author's own mental mood, and is therefore *honest.* The Science of Mind excludes opposites, and rests on unity.

It is proverbial that dishonesty retards spiritual growth and strikes at the heart of Truth. If a student at Harvard College has studied a textbook written by his teacher, is he entitled, when he leaves the University, to write out as his own the substance of this textbook? There is no warrant in common law and no permission in the gospel for plagiarizing an author's ideas and their words. Christian Science is not copyrighted; nor would protection by copyright be requisite, if mortals obeyed God's law of *manright*. A student can write voluminous works on Science without trespassing, if he writes honestly, and he cannot dishonestly compose *Christian Science*. The Bible is not stolen, though it is cited, and quoted deferentially.

Thoughts touched with the Spirit and Word of Christian Science gravitate naturally toward Truth. Therefore the mind to which this Science was revealed must have risen to the altitude which perceived a light beyond what others saw.

The spiritually minded meet on the stairs which lead up to spiritual love. This affection, so far from being personal worship, fulfils the law of Love which Paul enjoined upon the Galatians. This is the Mind "which was also in Christ Jesus," and knows no material limitations. It is the unity of good and bond of perfectness. This just affection serves to constitute the Mind-healer a wonder-worker,— as of old, on the Pentecost Day, when the disciples were of one accord.

He who gains the God-crowned summit of Christian Science never abuses the corporeal personality, but uplifts it. He thinks of every one in his real quality, and sees each mortal in an impersonal depict.

I have long remained silent on a growing evil in plagiarism; but if I do not insist upon the strictest observance of moral law and order in Christian Scientists, I become responsible, as a teacher, for laxity in discipline and lawlessness in literature. Pope was right in saying, "An honest man's the noblest work of God;" and Ingersoll's repartee has its moral: "An honest God's the noblest work of man."

Admonition

The neophyte in Christian Science acts like a diseased physique,— being too fast or too slow. He is inclined to do either too much or too little. In healing and teaching the student has not yet achieved the entire wisdom of Mind-practice. The textual explanation of this practice is complete in *Science and Health;* and scientific practice makes perfect, for it is governed by its Principle, and not by human opinions; but carnal and sinister motives, entering into this practice, will prevent the demonstration of Christian Science.

I recommend students not to read so-called scientific works, antagonistic to Christian Science, which advocate materialistic systems; because such works and words becloud the right sense of metaphysical Science.

The rules of Mind-healing are wholly Christlike and spiritual. Therefore the adoption of a worldly policy or a resort to subterfuge in the statement of the Science of Mind-healing, or any name given to it other than Christian Science, or an attempt to demonstrate the facts of this Science other than is stated in *Science and Health*—is a departure from the Science of Mind-healing. To becloud mortals, or for yourself to hide from God, is to conspire against the blessings otherwise conferred, against your own success and final happiness, against the progress of the human race as well as against *honest* metaphysical theory and practice.

Not by the hearing of the ear is spiritual truth learned and loved; nor cometh this apprehension from the experiences of others. We glean spiritual harvests from our own material losses. In this consuming heat false images are effaced from the canvas of mortal mind; and thus does the material pigment beneath fade into invisibility.

The signs for the wayfarer in divine Science lie in meekness, in unselfish motives and acts, in shuffling off scholastic rhetoric, in ridding the thought of effete doctrines, in the purification of the affections and desires.

Dishonesty, envy, and mad ambition are "lusts of the flesh," which uproot the germs of growth in Science and leave the inscrutable problem of being unsolved. Through the channels of material sense, of worldly policy, pomp, and pride, cometh no success in Truth. If beset with misguided emotions, we shall be stranded on the quicksands of worldly commotion, and practically come short of the wisdom requisite for teaching and demonstrating the victory over self and sin.

Be temperate in thought, word, and deed. Meekness and temperance are the jewels of Love, set in wisdom. Restrain untempered zeal. "Learn to labor and to wait." Of old the children of Israel were saved by patient waiting.

"The kingdom of heaven suffereth violence, and the violent take it by force!" said Jesus. Therefore are its spiritual gates not captured, nor its golden streets invaded.

We recognize this kingdom, the reign of harmony within us, by an unselfish affection or love, for this is the pledge of divine good and the insignia of heaven. This also is proverbial, that though eternal justice be graciously gentle, yet it may seem severe.

> For whom the Lord loveth He chasteneth,
> And scourgeth every son whom He receiveth.

As the poets in different languages have expressed it:—

> Though the mills of God grind slowly,
>   Yet they grind exceeding small;
> Though with patience He stands waiting,
>   With exactness grinds He all.

Though the divine rebuke is effectual to the pulling down of sin's strongholds, it may stir the human heart to resist Truth, before this heart becomes obediently receptive of the heavenly discipline. If the Christian Scientist recognize the mingled sternness and gentleness which permeate justice and Love, he will not scorn the timely reproof, but will so absorb it that this warning will be within him a spring, welling up into unceasing spiritual rise and progress. Patience and obedience win the golden scholarship of experimental tuition.

The kindly shepherd of the East carries his lambs in his arms to the sheepcot, but the older sheep pass into the fold under his compelling rod. He who sees the door and turns away from it, is guilty, while innocence strayeth yearningly.

There are no greater miracles known to earth than perfection and an unbroken friendship. We love our friends, but ofttimes we lose them in proportion to our affection. The sacrifices made for others are not infrequently met by envy, ingratitude, and enmity, which smite the heart and threaten to paralyze its beneficence. The unavailing tear is shed both for the living and the dead.

Nothing except sin, in the students themselves, can separate them from me. Therefore we should guard thought and action, keeping them in accord with Christ, and our friendship will surely continue.

The letter of the law of God, separated from its spirit, tends to demoralize mortals, and must be corrected by a diviner sense of liberty and light. The spirit of Truth extinguishes false thinking, feeling, and acting; and falsity must thus decay, ere spiritual sense, affectional consciousness, and genuine goodness become so apparent as to be well understood.

After the supreme advent of Truth in the heart, there comes an overwhelming sense of error's vacuity, of the blunders which arise from wrong apprehension. The enlightened heart loathes error, and casts it aside; or else that heart is consciously untrue to the light, faithless to itself and to others, and so sinks into deeper darkness. Said Jesus: "If the light that is in thee be darkness, how great is that darkness!" and Shakespeare puts this pious counsel into a father's mouth:—

> This above all: To thine own self be true;
> And it must follow, as the night the day,
> Thou canst not then be false to any man.

A realization of the shifting scenes of human happiness, and of the frailty of mortal anticipations,— such as first led me to the feet of Christian Science,— seems to be requisite at every stage of advancement. Though our first lessons are changed, modified, broadened, yet their core is constantly renewed; as the law of the chord remains unchanged, whether we are dealing with a simple Latour exercise or with the vast Wagner Trilogy.

A general rule is, that my students should not allow their movements to be controlled by other students, even if they are teachers and practitioners of the same blessed faith. The exception to this rule should be very rare.

The widest power and strongest growth have always been attained by those loyal students who rest on divine Principle for guidance, not on themselves; and who locate permanently in one section, and adhere to the orderly methods herein delineated.

At this period my students should locate in large cities, in order to do the greatest good to the greatest number, and therein abide. The population of our principal cities is ample to supply many practitioners, teachers, and preachers with work. This fact interferes in no way with the prosperity of each worker; rather does it represent an accumulation of power on his side which promotes the ease and welfare of the workers. Their liberated capacities of mind enable Christian Scientists to consummate much good or else evil; therefore their examples either excel or fall short of other religionists; and they must be found dwelling together in harmony, if even they compete with ecclesiastical fellowship and friendship.

It is often asked which revision of *Science and Health* is the best. The arrangement of my last revision, in 1890, makes the subject-matter clearer than any previous edition, and it is therefore better adapted to spiritualize thought and elucidate scientific healing and teaching. It has already been proven that this volume is accomplishing the divine purpose to a remarkable degree. The wise Christian Scientist will commend students

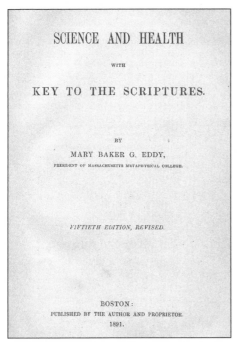

The fiftieth edition of *Science and Health with Key to the Scriptures*. This landmark edition was copyrighted in 1890 and published in 1891.

and patients to the teachings of this book, and the healing efficacy thereof, rather than try to centre their interest on himself.

Students whom I have taught are seldom benefited by the teachings of other students, for scientific foundations are already laid in their minds which ought not to be tampered with. Also, they are prepared to receive the infinite instructions afforded by the Bible and my books, which mislead no one and are their best guides.

The student may mistake in his conception of Truth, and this error, in an honest heart, is sure to be corrected. But if he misinterprets the text to his pupils, and communicates, even unintentionally, his misconception of Truth, thereafter he will find it more difficult to rekindle his own light or to enlighten them. Hence, as a rule, the student should explain only "Recapitulation," the chapter for the class-room, and leave *Science and Health* to God's daily interpretation.

Christian Scientists should take their textbook into the schoolroom the same as other teachers; they should ask questions from it, and be answered according to it,— occasionally reading aloud from the book to corroborate what they teach. It is also highly important that their pupils study each lesson before the recitation.

That these essential points are ever omitted, is anomalous, when we consider the necessity of thoroughly understanding Science, and the present liability of deviating from absolute Christian Science.

Centuries will intervene before the statement of the inexhaustible topics of *Science and Health* is sufficiently understood to be fully demonstrated.

The teacher himself should continue to study this textbook, and to spiritualize his own thoughts and human life from this open fount of Truth and Love.

He who sees clearly and enlightens other minds most readily, keeps his own lamp trimmed and burning. Throughout his entire explanations he strictly adheres to the teachings in the chapter on "Recapitulation." When closing the class, each member should own a copy of *Science and Health,* and continue to study and assimilate this inexhaustible subject— Christian Science.

The opinions of men cannot be substituted for God's revelation. In times past, arrogant pride, in attempting to steady the ark of Truth, obscured even the power and glory of the Scriptures,— to which *Science and Health* is the Key.

That teacher does most for his students who divests himself most of pride and self, and by reason thereof is able to empty his students' minds of error, that they may be filled with Truth. Thus doing, posterity will call him blessed, and the tired tongue of history be enriched.

The less the teacher personally controls other minds, and the more he trusts them to the divine Truth and Love, the better it will be for both teacher and student.

A teacher should take charge only of his own pupils and patients, and of those who voluntarily place themselves under his direction; he should avoid leaving his own regular institute or place of labor, or expending his labor where there are other teachers who should be specially responsible for doing their own work well.

Teachers of Christian Science will find it advisable to band together their students into associations, to continue the organization of churches, and at present they can employ any other organic operative method that may commend itself as useful to the Cause and beneficial to mankind.

Of this also rest assured, that books and teaching are but a ladder let down from the heaven of Truth and Love, upon which angelic thoughts ascend and descend, bearing on their pinions of light the Christ-spirit.

Guard yourselves against the subtly hidden suggestion that the Son of man will be glorified, or humanity benefited, by any deviation from the order prescribed by supernal grace. Seek to occupy no position whereto you do not feel that God ordains you. Never forsake your post without due deliberation and light, but always wait for God's finger to point the way. The loyal Christian Scientist is incapable alike of abusing the practice of Mind-healing or of healing on a material basis.

The tempter is vigilant, awaiting only an opportunity to divide the ranks of Christian Science and scatter the sheep abroad; but "if God be for us, who can be against us?" The Cause, *our* Cause, is highly prosperous, rapidly spreading over the globe; and the morrow will crown the effort of to-day with a diadem of gems from the New Jerusalem.

Exemplification

To energize wholesome spiritual warfare, to rebuke vainglory, to offset boastful emptiness, to crown patient toil, and rejoice in the spirit and power of Christian Science, we must ourselves be true. There is but one way of *doing* good, and that is to *do* it! There is but one way of *being* good, and that is to *be* good!

Art thou still unacquainted with thyself? Then be introduced to this self. "Know thyself!" as said the classic Grecian motto. Note well the falsity of this mortal self! Behold its vileness, and remember this poverty-stricken "stranger that is within thy gates." Cleanse every stain from this wanderer's soiled garments, wipe the dust from his feet and the tears from his eyes, that you may behold the real man, the fellow-saint of a holy household. There should be no blot on the escutcheon of our Christliness when we offer our gift upon the altar.

A student desiring growth in the knowledge of Truth, can and will obtain it by taking up his cross and following Truth. If he does this not, and another one undertakes to carry his burden and do his work, the duty will *not be accomplished*. No one can save himself without God's help, and God will help each man who performs his own part. After this manner and in no other way is every man cared for and blessed. To the unwise helper our Master said, "Follow me; and let the dead bury their dead."

The poet's line, "Order is heaven's first law," is so eternally true, so axiomatic, that it has become a truism; and its wisdom is as obvious in religion and scholarship as in astronomy or mathematics.

Experience has taught me that the rules of Christian Science can be far more thoroughly and readily acquired by regularly settled and systematic workers, than by unsettled and spasmodic efforts. Genuine Christian Scientists are, or should be, the most systematic and law-abiding people on earth, because their religion demands implicit adherence to fixed rules, in the orderly demonstration thereof. Let some of these rules be here stated.

First: Christian Scientists are to "heal the sick" as the Master commanded.

In so doing they must follow the divine order as prescribed by Jesus,— never, in any way, to trespass upon the rights of their neighbors, but to obey the celestial injunction, "Whatsoever ye would that men should do to you, do ye even so to them."

In this orderly, scientific dispensation healers become a law unto themselves. They feel their own burdens less, and can therefore bear the weight of others' burdens, since it is only through the lens of their unselfishness that the sunshine of Truth beams with such efficacy as to dissolve error.

It is already understood that Christian Scientists will not receive a patient who is under the care of a regular physician, until he has done with the case and different aid is sought. The same courtesy should be observed in the professional intercourse of Christian Science healers with one another.

Second: Another command of the Christ, his prime command, was that his followers should "raise the dead." He lifted his own body from the sepulchre. In him, Truth called the physical man from the tomb to health, and the so-called dead forthwith emerged into a higher manifestation of Life.

The spiritual significance of this command, "Raise the dead," most concerns mankind. It implies such an elevation of the understanding as will enable thought to apprehend the living beauty of Love, its practicality, its divine energies, its health-giving and life-bestowing qualities,— yea, its power to demonstrate immortality. This end Jesus achieved, both by example and precept.

Third: This leads inevitably to a consideration of another part of Christian Science work,— a part which concerns us intimately,— preaching the gospel.

This evangelistic duty should not be so warped as to signify that we must or may go, uninvited, to work in other vineyards than our own. One would, or should, blush to enter unasked another's pulpit, and preach without the consent of the stated occupant of that pulpit. The Lord's command means this, that we should adopt the spirit of the Saviour's ministry, and abide in such a spiritual attitude as will draw men unto us. Itinerancy should not be allowed to clip the wings of divine Science. Mind demonstrates omnipresence and omnipotence, but Mind revolves on a spiritual axis, and its power is displayed and its presence felt in eternal stillness and immovable Love. The divine potency of this spiritual mode of Mind, and the hindrance opposed to it by material motion, is proven beyond a doubt in the practice of Mind-healing.

In those days preaching and teaching were substantially one. There was no church preaching, in the modern sense of the term. Men assembled in the one temple (at Jerusalem) for sacrificial ceremonies, not for sermons. Into the synagogues, scattered about in cities and villages, they went for liturgical worship, and instruction in the Mosaic law. If one worshipper preached to the others, he did so informally, and because he was bidden to this privileged duty at that particular moment. It was the custom to pay this hortatory compliment to a stranger, or to a member who had been away from the neighborhood; as Jesus was once asked to exhort, when he had been some time absent from Nazareth but once again entered the synagogue which he had frequented in childhood.

Jesus' method was to instruct his own students; and he watched and guarded them unto the end, even according to his promise, "Lo, I am with you alway!" Nowhere in the four Gospels will Christian Scientists find any precedent for employing another student to take charge of their students, or for neglecting their own students, in order to enlarge their sphere of action.

Above all, trespass not intentionally upon other people's thoughts, by endeavoring to influence other minds to any action not first made known to them or sought by them. Corporeal and selfish influence is human, fallible, and temporary; but incorporeal impulsion is divine, infallible, and eternal. The student should be most careful not to thrust aside Science, and shade God's window which lets in light, or seek to stand in God's stead.

Does the faithful shepherd forsake the lambs,— retaining his salary for tending the home flock while he is serving another fold? There is no evidence to show that Jesus ever entered the towns whither he sent his disciples; no evidence that he there taught a few hungry ones, and then left them to starve or to stray. To these selected ones (like "the elect lady" to whom St. John addressed one of his epistles) he gave personal instruction, and gave in plain words, until they were able to fulfil his behest and depart on their united pilgrimages. This he did, even though one of the twelve whom he kept near himself betrayed him, and others forsook him.

The true mother never willingly neglects her children in their early and sacred hours, consigning them to the care of nurse or stranger. Who can feel and comprehend the needs of her babe like the ardent mother? What other heart yearns with her solicitude, endures with her patience, waits with her hope, and labors with her love, to promote the welfare and happiness of her children? Thus must the Mother in Israel give all her hours to those first sacred tasks, till her children can walk steadfastly in wisdom's ways.

One of my students wrote to me: "I believe the proper thing for us to do is to follow, as nearly as we can, in the path you have pursued!" It is gladdening to find, in such a student, one of the children of light. It is safe to leave with God the government of man. He appoints and He anoints His Truth-bearers, and God is their sure defense and refuge.

The parable of "the prodigal son" is rightly called "the pearl of parables," and our Master's greatest utterance may well be called "the diamond sermon." No purer and more exalted teachings ever fell upon human ears than those contained in what is commonly known as the Sermon on the Mount,— though this name has been given it by compilers and translators of the Bible, and not by the Master himself or by the Scripture authors. Indeed, this title really indicates more the Master's mood, than the material locality.

Where did Jesus deliver this great lesson—or, rather, this series of great lessons—on humanity and divinity? On a hillside, near the sloping shores of the Lake of Galilee, where he spake primarily to his immediate disciples.

In this simplicity, and with such fidelity, we see Jesus ministering to the spiritual needs of all who placed themselves under his care, always leading them into the divine order, under the sway of his own perfect understanding. His power over others was spiritual, not corporeal. To the students whom he had chosen, his immortal teaching was the bread of Life. When *he* was with them, a fishing-boat became a sanctuary, and the solitude was peopled with holy messages from the All-Father. The grove became his class-room, and nature's haunts were the Messiah's university.

What has this hillside priest, this seaside teacher, done for the human race? Ask, rather, what has he *not* done. His holy humility, unworldliness, and self-abandonment wrought infinite results. The method of his religion was not too simple to be sublime, nor was his power so exalted as to be unavailable for the needs of suffering mortals, whose wounds he healed by Truth and Love.

His order of ministration was "first the blade, then the ear, after that the full corn in the ear." May we unloose the latchets of his Christliness, inherit his legacy of love, and reach the fruition of his promise: "If ye abide in me, and my words abide in you, ye shall ask what ye will, and it shall be done unto you."

Waymarks

In the first century of the Christian era Jesus went about doing good. The evangelists of those days wandered about. Christ, or the spiritual idea, appeared to human consciousness as the man Jesus. At the present epoch the human concept of Christ is based on the incorporeal divine Principle of man, and Science has elevated this idea and established its rules in consonance with their Principle. Hear this saying of our Master, "And I, if I be lifted up from the earth, will draw all men unto me."

The ideal of God is no longer impersonated as a waif or wanderer; and Truth is not fragmentary, disconnected, unsystematic, but concentrated and immovably fixed in Principle. The best spiritual type of Christly method for uplifting human thought and imparting divine Truth, is stationary power, stillness, and strength; and when this spiritual ideal is made our own, it becomes the model for human action.

St. Paul said to the Athenians, "For in Him we live, and move, and have our being." This statement is in substance identical with my own: "There is no life, truth, substance, nor intelligence in matter." It is quite clear that as yet this grandest verity has not been fully demonstrated, but it is nevertheless true. If Christian Science reiterates St. Paul's teaching, we, as Christian Scientists, should give to the world convincing proof of the validity of this scientific statement of being. Having perceived, in advance of others, this scientific fact, we owe to ourselves and to the world a struggle for its demonstration.

At some period and in some way the conclusion must be met that whatsoever seems true, and yet contradicts divine Science and St. Paul's text, must be and is false; and that whatsoever seems to be good, and yet errs, though acknowledging the true way, is really evil.

As dross is separated from gold, so Christ's baptism of fire, his purification through suffering, consumes whatsoever is of sin. Therefore this purgation of divine mercy, destroying all error, leaves no flesh, no matter, to the mental consciousness.

When all fleshly belief is annihilated, and every spot and blemish on the disk of consciousness is removed, then, and not till then, will immortal Truth be found true, and scientific teaching, preaching, and practice be essentially one. "Happy is he that condemneth not himself in that thing which he alloweth. . . . for whatsoever is not of faith is sin." (Romans xiv. 22, 23.)

There is no "lo here! or lo there!" in divine Science; its manifestation must be "the same yesterday, and to-day, and forever," since Science is eternally one, and unchanging, in Principle, rule, and demonstration.

I am persuaded that only by the modesty and distinguishing affection illustrated in Jesus' career, can Christian Scientists aid the establishment of Christ's kingdom on the earth. In the first century of the Christian era Jesus' teachings bore much fruit, and the Father was glorified therein. In this period and the forthcoming centuries, watered by dews of divine Science, this "tree of life" will blossom into greater freedom, and its leaves will be "for the healing of the nations."

Ask God to give thee skill
In comfort's art:
That thou may'st consecrated be
And set apart
Unto a life of sympathy.
For heavy is the weight of ill
In every heart;
And comforters are needed much
Of Christlike touch.
— A. E. Hamilton

Footprints Fadeless

by MARY BAKER EDDY

To

the patient, glad, toilers

in the vineyard of our Lord,

I lovingly dedicate my

Footprints.

MARY BAKER G. EDDY

Footprints, that perhaps another,
Sailing o'er life's solemn main,
A forlorn and shipwrecked brother,
Seeing, shall take heart again.
LONGFELLOW — *A Psalm of Life*

Oh sometimes gleams upon our sight,
Through present wrongs, the eternal Right;
And step by step, since time began,
We see the steady gain of man.
WHITTIER — *Old and New*

A Significant Life

I have been asked so frequently for the names of my first students, and for jottings from the early history of Christian Science, that my first spare moments are employed to copy briefly from old manuscripts, prints, letters, and from memory, the following incidents in the course of my experience of the re-birth of an idea which vibrates in unison with divine order.

Very early in life there was a demand for my literary productions.[82] When about eighteen years of age, I wrote for the *Belknap Gazette,* published in New Hampshire, and later for the *New Hampshire Patriot.* After an academic course, I graduated under Professor Dyer H. Sanborn, the celebrated author of *Sanborn's Grammar.* Later I wrote for the leading magazines of the South, and on my return to the North after the death of my beloved husband, Colonel Glover, I was offered an annual salary of $3,000 by the editor of the *Odd Fellows'* magazine, published by the U.S. Lodge. Other leading magazines both North and South have allowed me to name my salary, and never objected to paying it.

If all my poems from early years which have appeared in public print were collected, they would fill a good-sized volume. My *Miscellaneous Writings,* gathered in book form in 1896, has passed its 42nd edition of one thousand copies each; and the Christian Science textbook, *Science and Health with Key to the Scriptures,* of which I am the author, has reached its 225th edition of a thousand copies each.

I have lectured in large crowded halls at Portland and Waterville, Maine; Boston, Massachusetts; Providence, Rhode Island; New York City; Washington, D.C.; and Chicago.

In 1846 the Rev. Richard S. Rust, D.D., at that time principal of the Methodist Conference Seminary, in Northfield, New Hampshire, asked me to supply the place of his principal female teacher during her absence for a few weeks. Among other pleasant memories of that occasion, I recall entering a classroom one day and finding on the blackboard a fine compliment "to Mrs. Glover," written by the professor.

Col. George W. Glover

The only known likeness of George Washington Glover, the first husband of Mary Baker Eddy, date unknown. He married Mary Baker on December 10, 1843.

My first husband, Col. George W. Glover, of Charleston, South Carolina, was at Wilmington, North Carolina, attending to business, when he was seized with yellow fever and died in that city. I was with him, watched day and night at his bedside in speechless woe, till he passed the dark shadow. My name was his last word. The interest manifested in his recovery by the Free Masons and the citizens was unsurpassed. He was a Royal Arch Mason, and buried with Masonic honors. A great procession followed his remains. His body was not allowed to be taken to our beautiful home in Charleston, South Carolina, owing to fear of contagion, but marked respect and affection were bestowed to his memory. The Wilmington city officials took possession of the body. The lodge and chapter of which he was a member, in Charleston, South Carolina, passed resolutions of sorrow and condolence, and wore the usual badge of mourning. He was a Master Mason in St. Andrews Lodge No. 10 of Charleston, South Carolina.

On my departure for the North, the Governor of the State and his staff, together with the Rev. Repiton, an Episcopal clergyman, and other Free Masons, attended me to the station, and engaged a Brother Mason to accompany me to my father's home in New Hampshire, giving him strict charge concerning my safety and comfort during the journey.

My husband was said to own much property in slaves;[83] but I did not sell them after his decease. Although agreeing with Southrons as to racial distinction, such as nature constitutes, yet I never could feel that I owned property in a human being.

The following is a brief extract from a glowing tribute to Colonel Glover, which appeared in the *Masonic Magazine:*

> He was devotedly attached to Masonry,[84] faithful as a member and officer of the Lodge and Chapter, and beloved by his brothers and companions, who mourned his early death.
>
> He had been instructed "how to live" and "how to die," and that instruction had been sealed to his heart. He departed in hope and peace.
>
> He was *our Brother;* he has gone at the call of *our Father.* Although we lament his departure from the terrestrial Lodge, we trust we shall meet him in the Celestial Grand Lodge, when our *work* shall be perfect—our refreshments divine.

A Distinguished Dentist

My second husband, Daniel Patterson, D.D.S., was appointed by Governor Berry of New Hampshire to go to the South and disburse to loyal Southerners some government fees. Dr. Patterson was not a soldier, but a citizen prisoner.[85]

In 1873, while he was in Littleton, New Hampshire, I obtained a divorce from him for adultery. Mr. R. D. Rounsevel, proprietor of the White Mountain House, White Mountains, New Hampshire, writes:

Daniel Patterson, the second husband of Mary Baker Eddy, probably in the 1860s. He married the widowed Mary Baker Glover on June 21, 1853. From a visiting card in Eddy's photograph album.

About the year 1874, Dr. Daniel Patterson, a dentist, boarded with me in Littleton, New Hampshire. During his stay at different times I had conversation with him about his wife, from whom he was separated. He spoke of her as being a pure and Christian woman, and that the cause of the separation was wholly on his part; that if he had done as he ought, he might have had as pleasant and happy a home as one could wish for.

At that time I had no knowledge of who his wife was. Later on I learned that Mary Baker G. Eddy, the discoverer and founder of Christian Science, was the above-mentioned woman.

R. D. Rounsevel
January 18, 1902

Mental Healing in the Fifties

In the fifties, Mrs. Smith, of Rumney, New Hampshire, came to me with her infant, whose eyes were diseased, a mass of inflammation, neither pupil nor iris discernable. I gave the infant no drugs, held her in my arms a few moments while lifting my thoughts to God, then returned the babe to her mother healed. In grateful memory thereof, Mrs. Smith named her babe Mary and embroidered a petticoat for me. I have carefully preserved that garment to this day.

This simple case of mental healing occurred in the fifties, before I saw P. P. Quimby, and before I gave up the practice of homoeopathy on the conviction that mind, more than matter, is the Esculapius.

I would limit my philanthropy sooner than harm a child. The children are blest above others by Christian Science. It heals them sooner than it can adults; it relieves them from nauseous lotions and big pills. They become good healers sooner than do adults, for they are nearer the kingdom of heaven. The child of seven years old may become the family physician. It is the children's native element; in it they revel in the liberty of health and divine Love. Let the children speak for themselves on this subject.

Gen. Benjamin F. Butler's Letter

I here quote an interesting correspondence which passed between Gen. Benjamin F. Butler and myself in 1861. The General's original letter is in my possession.

Rumney, N.H.
August 17, 1861

General Benjamin F. Butler

My dear Sir:

Permit me individually, and as the representative of thousands of my sex in your native state, to tender the homage and gratitude due to you, one of her noblest sons, who so bravely vindicated the claims of humanity in your late letter to Secretary Cameron. You dared to assume, in the dignity of defending with your latest breath our country's honor, a position of justice and equity. The final solution of the great National query, Will freedom be rendered to black as well as white—men, women, and children—whom you have the courage and honor to defend in this the hour of our country's pain and purification?, must soon follow.

You hold freedom to be the normal condition of those made in God's image: so do we all. In this, the man can only equal the soldier who offers his life for his country, and by fairness of argument elucidates the justice which will surely transmit to posterity the success of a republican form of government, in heritage perpetual, undimmed in its lustre. The red strife between right and wrong will be fierce, but it cannot be long, and victory on the side of immutable justice will be well worth its cost.

But I will not task your time or forbearance farther. Your act has thrilled with electric hope the homes and hearts of this section of our country, hope in God and in the Right. Give us in the field and on the forum men like our brave "Ben. Butler," and our country is saved.

Respectfully,

Mary M. Patterson

To this letter General Butler responded in the following words:

Headquarters Department of Virginia

Mary M. Patterson
Rumney, N.H.

Madame:

In reply to your favor of the 12th inst., I am directed by the General in command to express the thousand obligations he is under for your kind expressions, sympathy, and consideration.

The discharge of public duty is made easy by such commendation, coming from the noble and the loyal of the land.

I have the honor to be
Very respectfully
Your servant,

P. Hagerty
Aide-de-camp to
Maj. Gen. Butler

About the year 1863 I lectured at Waterville College, in Maine, on the subject "North and South." Professor Sheldon paid me a high compliment through the newspapers, and the boys in blue serenaded me. It was an occasion not to be forgotten.

A Magnetic Doctor

In 1862 I went from a hydropathic institute to Dr. P. P. Quimby, a magnetic physician.[86] He used no drugs; with this exception, his method in no way related to Christian Science. He never intimated to me in two years that he treated the sick metaphysically. He did not pray for me when treating me; he talked with me on various subjects, then wet his hands in water and manipulated my head. He helped me for a while, but failed to cure me. He had almost no book-learning, but advanced views on his subject of magnetic practice. He was not scientific; he was not a Christian Scientist. My complete departure from his practice is proven in that the first students in Christian Science tried to demonstrate my teachings after Quimby's method, but Christian Science could neither be demonstrated thus, nor by any material method. Christ was, and is, my only teacher of Christian Science.

We have no record that Jesus described disease, but he healed it. I taught students in Christian Science not to describe disease, but to heal it. Whereas Mr. Quimby, after manipulating his patients, retired to record a description of the person and of the disease. I once asked him to show me his description of my case; I read it and returned it to him.

While under Mr. Quimby's treatment, he frequently asked me to look over his scribblings and put them in grammatical form. This I did. Also I wrote manuscript copies of my own and left them with him. I had no occasion or incentive to steal his thunder.

My first student will say I never taught him what is contained in the chapter "Recapitulation," in *Science and Health.* I failed to fully state Christian Science until I had written *Science and Health,* in 1875, nine years after the death of Mr. Quimby. *The Science of Man* was written in

Phineas Parkhurst Quimby (1802–1866), the "magnetic doctor" from Maine. From a visiting card in Eddy's photograph album.

Lynn, about 1870. It was my own composition, and I prepared it for a class I taught.

In what I wrote, I sought to express what I had discovered, but failing at first to do this, learned to "labor and to wait" for more fitness to express an awakened spiritual sense of what the infinite subject of Christian Science contains. I could not have written *Science and Health with*

Key to the Scriptures sooner than I did. Ask any loyal student to-day if he could learn Christian Science, as I now teach it, from the manuscripts I wrote for my first student, or if he could demonstrate it by manipulation or by electricity. What would his answer be? This is my proof that Mr. Quimby's scribblings, and his treatment of the sick, were mental leagues apart from Christian Science. I refer to these facts in my preface to *Science and Health with Key to the Scriptures.*

The copies that I have seen purporting to be originally his are chiefly plagiarisms from my private manuscripts and copyrighted works.

Quimby believed that matter is as real as Spirit, and that sin, disease, death, and contagion are *real.* In Christian Science, all is Spirit and spiritual; there is no matter, no contagion, sin, disease, death — God is All in all, infinite. And the infinite can know nothing and cause nothing apart from the nature of the infinite.

I had dropped this subject, relating to a fossilized falsehood. But evidence and testimony on the side of Truth are always in order, and proverbially better late than never. Hence I republish from *The Christian Science Journal* an extract from the following letter[87] mailed to me by a student:

Mary H. Philbrick (1832–1906). Introduced to Christian Science in Chicago, Philbrick studied with Mary Baker Eddy in 1884, 1886, and 1888. A nineteenth-century cabinet card photograph.

It might be interesting for you to know that Mr. A. J. Swartz, of Chicago, went to see the late Dr. P. P. Quimby's son, and procured his father's writings for the purpose of having them published in order to show the world that your ideas were borrowed from Quimby. After having examined them, it was found there was nothing that would compare in any way to *Science and Health;* and he concluded that it would aid you too much to publish them, so they were returned to the owner.

Mrs. Swartz saw and read these manuscripts and she gave me this information.

Mary H. Philbrick
Austin, Ill.
May 18, 1892

The following letter is republished from *The Christian Science Journal* of November, 1886, an attested statement in reference to Dr. Quimby's method of healing the sick:

I was treated by Dr. P. P. Quimby, in Portland, for neuralgia in the head. Mrs. Eddy was also a patient of his. I first met her there, and it was in the summer of 1862. His mode of treating the sick was to immerse his hands in water and manipulate their heads. My father (W. P. Morgan) offered him one thousand dollars ($1,000) to explain his method of treating disease; to which the doctor replied, "I cannot; I do not understand it myself." I never knew of his attempting to teach any one. His method was entirely different from Mrs. Eddy's system of Christian Science.

(Witness) Mrs. E. A. Thompson
We concur in affirming the known truth of the above statement.

Mrs. A. D. Morgan
W. P. Morgan, A.M.
Mrs. A. R. Rutten
Minneapolis, Minnesota
September, 1886

I wish to add to the above statement that I was acquainted with Mr. Quimby four years, and I never heard him say that God healed his patients. He gave me no spiritual explanation of the Scriptures, while Mrs. Eddy's teachings and writings contain little else. I first met Mrs. Mary Baker G. Eddy in Dr. Quimby's office at the hotel in Portland, Me.—he was not a teacher of her method, neither did he use the pathological system originated by her. In 1886, Mrs. Eddy taught me Christian Science, and she taught me to overcome evil with good, never to harm others. I have practised Christian Science fifteen years; and I know it to be as far above that which Mr. Quimby talked, wrote, and practised as the heavens are above the earth. I did not regain my health until after I learned Christian Science.

Emma A. Thompson

Emma A. Thompson (1842–1913). Thompson first met Mary Baker Eddy in 1862 in Portland, Maine, where both women were patients of Phineas Parkhurst Quimby. Thompson eventually became a Christian Scientist and studied with Eddy in 1886, 1887, and 1898.

The following offer first appeared in the *Boston Post* and the *Boston Traveler* in 1887. It has never been accepted.

To Whom it May Concern:

Mr. George A. Quimby, son of the late Phineas P. Quimby, over his own signature and before witness, stated in 1883 that he had in his possession at that time all the manuscripts that had been written by his father. And I hereby declare that, to expose the falsehood of parties intimating that I have appropriated matter belonging to the aforesaid Quimby, I will pay the cost of printing and publishing the first edition of those manuscripts with the author's name.

Provided, that I am allowed first to examine said manuscripts, and do find that they were his own compositions, and not mine, that were left with him many years ago, or that they have not since his death, in 1866, been stolen from my published works. Also that I am given the right to bring out this one edition under the copyright of the owner of said manuscripts, and all the money accruing from the sales of said book shall be paid to said owner. Some of his purported writings, quoted by Mr. D[resser], were my own words, as near as I can recollect them.

There is a great demand for my work *Science and Health with Key to the Scriptures;* hence Mr. D[resser]'s excuse for the delay to publish Quimby's manuscripts, namely, that this period is not sufficiently enlightened to be benefitted by them, is lost, for if I have copied from Quimby, and my book is accepted, it has created a demand for his.

Mary Baker G. Eddy
Boston Traveler
May 21, 1887

When I knew him, Mr. Quimby had not learned the Psalmist's "secret" of health and holiness; but we trust he now knows it and is the redeemed of divine Love. Many were his virtues; let us tread lightly on his ashes.

Mrs. Mary A. Baker's Letter

Mrs. Baker is the widow of my oldest brother; her maiden name was Cook. She was the Mary A. Cook who wrote the *History of the Judsons,* and was often referred to with approval in the *Missionary Herald*—her whole life is a grand psalm. She writes as follows:

Rev. Irving C. Tomlinson
Concord, N.H.

Dear Sir:

At this time, when so much is being said in public most appreciatively of the Rev. Mary Baker G. Eddy, discoverer and founder of Christian Science, and also somewhat that is untruthful, absurd, and wholly unchristian, I desire to make the following statement:

First, I will say that I am not a Christian Scientist, but am of the Orthodox faith, and for more than half a century have been a member of the Park Street Congregational Church in Boston, Mass. My beloved husband, long since passed to his rest, was Mrs. Eddy's oldest brother, and I know the facts of her life as no one can know them who is not thus allied in kinship and family history. The church and faith that were ours were hers also until 1866.

Her early bereavement was followed by a long illness, when failing to be healed by medical skill, she felt there must be something outside the ordinary methods of healing. After much study of the Bible, for which she isolated herself for years, she came to the conclusion, "It is God that does all." Acting on this faith she was able through divine help to recover her health.

It is not strange, in view of the frequency of failure by the medical fraternity to restore their patients to health, that other means should be sought. While I am not a believer in the entirety of Christian Science, I do believe that God is able to heal us physically and spiritually, if we confide in His love and trust in Him for all our needs. Whether logical as truth, or otherwise, Christian Science is her faith, sincerely embraced after long years of faithful study of the Bible; and according to her belief it is intelligently taught. She is now, and has been for thirty-five years, hard at work in the cause she espoused. With her means she is carrying blessings to many a needy one, and she works on seeking the good of all. Whatever differences of belief the public may entertain concerning any of her doctrines, they cannot justly ignore the fact that hers is an earnest, generous, and noble life—the legitimate outgrowth of a noble soul.

Mary Ann Cook Baker (1830–1902). The second wife of Mary Baker Eddy's brother Samuel, Mary Ann Cook Baker had been a missionary to Native Americans and was a longtime friend to Eddy.

Mrs. Eddy's character is above reproach. No libelous words can touch it, no foe can assail it. Hidden in God it shall shine, and, reflecting Him, its brilliancy will be seen long after she who labors ceases her work for ultimate rest. Her large and extensive work, with her unprecedented following, has called forth malignant utterances so utterly false they should not go unchallenged.

I am acquainted with the birth and growth of Christian Science, and know that the claim that it originated with Phineas P. Quimby is absurd, and without foundation. I can state positively that Mrs. Eddy never received any instructions or suggestions from him in regard to Metaphysical healing or Christian Science. I know whereof I speak, because I accompanied her to Dr. Quimby; at that time she was too feeble to go unattended. His treatment consisted of manipulations in cold water, and was wholly material, and entirely devoid of metaphysics or spirituality. Both my husband and myself made careful inquiries in regard to Mr. Quimby's system of treatment while Mrs. Eddy was under his care, and we considered his methods to be the essence of quackery.

I also desire to say most emphatically that my sister, Mrs. Eddy, never was a spiritualist. She never held a spiritualistic séance in Boston, or anywhere else. I have known her for fifty years, and I know that all the charges brought against her are the work of ignorance and malice, and wholly devoid of any semblance of fact. Her great kindness to me can never be forgotten. I pray God to sustain her and keep her from all harm. A difference in theological views does not call for such treatment as she has received from some who disagree with her.

My standing in the Orthodox Church will vouch for the truth of every word I have written in this letter. Perhaps I should say that I was educated for missionary work, and early became a member of the American Board of Commissioners of Foreign Missions. I went out as a missionary to labor among the Choctaw Indians at Pine Ridge Seminary, Indian Territory, where I was Principal of that institution. I continued in the missionary field of labor until the failure of my health. In these many years of Christian activity I was associated with Rev. I. C. Strong and wife, Revs. Kingsbury and Hotchkins, and other well known Christian workers.

Under great trial and persecution, I feel that Mrs. Eddy has been true to these words, which I select from one of her poems:

> Oh! Make me glad for every scalding tear,
>   For hope deferred, ingratitude, disdain!
> Wait, and love more for every hate, and fear
>   No ill,—since God is good, and loss is gain.

Her whole life has been a beautiful exponent of these words from her poem entitled "Christ My Refuge," which I select from a multiplicity of kindred thoughts found in her literary works:

> My prayer, some daily good to do
>   To Thine for Thee;
> An offering pure of Love, whereto
>   God leadeth me.

I have written to you in the interest of Christianity regarding personally known facts—Christianity, whose foundation stones are righteousness, justice, and truth—with the prayer that only the right may triumph.

Mary A. Baker
Boston, Mass.
August 20, 1901

First Student a Living Witness

My first student in Christian Science was Mr. Hiram S. Crafts, of Stoughton, Massachusetts. I taught him in Lynn, Massachusetts, in 1867; afterward he returned to his home in Stoughton, and his wife urgently wrote to me to come to them and help her husband commence practice. I went and remained there about one year, left him with a good practice, and gave him his tuition.

Mr. Crafts speaks thereof as follows:

I hereby certify that Mrs. Mary Baker G. Eddy, the discoverer and founder of Christian Science, was not a spiritualist when she taught me Christian Science in the year 1867. At that date I was a spiritualist, but her teachings changed my views on that subject, and I gave up spiritualism. Mrs. Eddy boarded at my house when I resided in Stoughton, Massachusetts. She furnished our parlor, and gave us the use of her furniture free of cost while she remained with us.

She never taught me in my mental practice to hurt others, but only to heal the sick and reform the sinner. She taught me from the Scriptures, and from manuscripts that she wrote as she taught me.

Hiram Crafts (1836–1906). A shoe-maker, Hiram Crafts was the first student of Mary Baker Eddy. During the time she boarded with the Crafts family (1866–1867), he briefly prac-ticed spiritual healing. A tintype.

Hiram S. Crafts
Concord, N.H.
December 14, 1901

My third student was Mrs. Sally Wentworth, of Stoughton, Massachusetts. She, her husband, Mr. Alanson C. Wentworth, and their daughter Celia have passed away; hence I have not their testimony on the above subject, which I doubt not they would gladly give—but I have letters in their own handwriting which show our mutually friendly attitude, both before and after I left them. Mr. Crafts's and Mrs. Wentworth's were my only boarding places in Stoughton. I had no acquaintances during my short stay there except the patients of the aforesaid students. The neighbors at that time were not near, and if I had occasion to go out in the evening some member of the above-named families always accompanied me.

After returning to Lynn, Mrs. Wentworth wrote requesting me to come to Stoughton and teach her Christian Science. In due time I went there. When I was ready to leave them, she told me that she earned from her practice $50 per week.

I taught Mrs. Wentworth Christian Science more from sympathy than for money, for she had told me that owing to her husband's long illness and inability to work they were poor. My terms for her tuition were a small percentage on her practice. But I made no demands for this, and took no *legal action* to obtain it.

When I was ready to return to Lynn, Mr. Wentworth took me to the depot, and thanked me cordially for what I had done for him and his family. On my arrival in Lynn, when unpacking my trunk I missed some articles I had forgotten, and had left in the closet in the chamber that I occupied. I informed Mrs. Wentworth of it, naming the articles (one was a pair of boots), and requested her to send them to me at her earliest convenience. She sent them in *good condition.* The floor in my room was not carpeted; pretty homemade rugs cheered it.

After I left them I received the following certificate and letters in their own handwriting, the originals of which I possess:

I cheerfully give my testimonial to the wonderful efficacy of the Science Mrs. Glover teaches, in its application to my case. I was the melancholy victim of sciatica in the hip for many long years; at times I could neither lie, sit, or stand without great suffering. When I first saw Mrs. Glover she told me she could cure me; but I must say it seemed impossible, after suffering so long and trying so many things, that I could be healed without medicine or application of any sort. Yet such was the case. After she had conversed with me I improved until my hip disease left me, and I am completely rid of it.

Alanson C. Wentworth

Stoughton, Mass.

1873

I was also cured of an inveterate habit of smoking and chewing tobacco.

A. C. Wentworth

The following is the daughter's letter:

Stoughton

March 16, 1868

Dear Mrs. Patterson:

We received your letter February 6th. Father and mother have been teasing me to write to you ever since. I am ashamed because I have not written before. I read your letter before breakfast, then sat up and ate and drank with the rest and have ever since; before that I had been living on toasted bread and going all day without drink. You don't know how much good your letter did me. How can I ever pay you for all you have done for me? I will send you some money in this letter, but that won't begin to pay you, but it is the best I can do this time. Mother said if I would begin a letter she would finish it, so I leave the rest for her to write.

Yours with love,
Celia

Dear Mrs. Patterson:

I will tell you all the news I can think of. Hiram Crafts and wife made us a call last Sunday. He says he has not given up doctoring. James Atherton's wife is dead, funeral yesterday. Mrs. Holbrook and daughter are well. E. Brigg's stable was burnt a few weeks ago. E. Tucker's shop was burnt two weeks since, another house owned by the Irish in the same neighborhood, all burned to the ground. Three other buildings were set on fire, but extinguished before much damage was done. Folks think there is danger of being burnt out to live in Stoughton Corner. We see C. A. French almost every week; he is quite smart; he thinks coming here does him good. We all feel very thankful to you. Your letters do us a great deal of good.

S. Wentworth

Upon severing my connection with my dear old church in Tilton, New Hampshire, I received the following letter of dismissal from my pastor:

June 13, 1875

This certifies that Mrs. Mary M. Glover is a member of this Church in good and regular standing. At her own request she is dismissed from this and recommended to any evangelical Church in Lynn.

When received there her particular connection with us will cease.

Theodore C. Pratt
Pastor of Congregational Church
Tilton, N.H.

The Wentworth home in Stoughton, Massachusetts. Mary Baker Eddy boarded with the Wentworths for eighteen months between 1868 and 1870 and taught Sally Wentworth her method of spiritual healing.

In 1877 I married Mr. Asa G. Eddy and in 1878 was called to preach in Boston at the Baptist Tabernacle of the Rev. Daniel C. Eddy, D.D., by the pastor of that church, the Rev. Joseph Williams. I accepted the call and during my ministry there the congregation so increased in number that the pews were not sufficient to seat the audience and benches were used in the aisles.

The following is my certificate of ordination as pastor of the *first* Church in the Christian Science denomination:

This certifies that Mrs. Mary B. G. Eddy was ordained Pastor of the "Church of Christ," chartered in Massachusetts, 1879. She preached for us three years, and we reverence her Christian character and great ability to preach the gospel. While she was with us she built up the Church and society to a flourishing condition, and it is with a sincere sense of our obligations to her, and with the most tender regrets, that we give her up to enter upon new tasks.

Per order of the Church

H. P. Smith
Clerk
Boston
Dec. 28th, 1880

Previous to my ordination I had preached for the aforesaid society three years.

Very sacred to me are the memories that cluster around my old home, the city of Lynn, bordering the birthplace of Christian Science. Through the generosity and thoughtfulness of the citizens of Lynn, the earthly dwelling where *Science and Health with Key to the Scriptures* was written—where my husband, Dr. Eddy, and I instituted the Christian Scientists Home, and passed many happy hours in prayer to God and work for man—has been purchased and set apart as a memorial to those fruitful labors for the upbuilding of humanity.

Stages of Advancement

After I had made the discovery in 1866 that All is Mind; there is no matter; that Mind includes all that is real of man and the universe, this infinite subject had to be mentally digested and its method of practice comprehended by students before I could give it to the public in a book. So immature was the general thought upon this topic, I did not venture to print my manuscript of Christian Science for several years after its discovery. Some of my first students waited to grow to the stature of my teaching and practice. These now can heal through prayer, for they understand that the sick are healed by the divine power, and by spiritual means wherein matter has no part.

From 1866 to 1875, I myself was learning Christian Science step by step—gradually developing the wonderful germ I had discovered as an honest investigator. It was practical evolution. I was reaching by experience and demonstration the scientific proof, and scientific statement, of what I had already discovered. My later teachings and writings show the steady growth of my spiritual ideal during those pregnant years.

After teaching my first class in Christian Science, the fact was proven that its demonstration rests wholly on a spiritual basis. Thereafter my students conformed to this rule.

I have faced the destiny of a discoverer and pioneer from first to last, had to unfold gradually the divine mystery—open to all, but seen by almost none, according to His word.

The method of practice for students perplexed me. Although I healed through spiritual power—the divine influx of Truth—students could not be taught up to the silent effectual prayer that casts out evils and heals the sick till they received the unction of the Spirit. This was as impracticable

Major revisions of *Science and Health with Key to the Scriptures*. These milestones in the publishing history of *Science and Health* include the first (1875), second (1878), third (1881), sixth (1883), sixteenth (1886), fiftieth (1891), 226th (1902), and the 1907 editions.

as for a clergyman to make a sinner pray for himself effectually until he is moved by divine Spirit to seek salvation. A preparation of the heart or the individual consciousness is requisite in both cases.

In my revisions of *Science and Health*, its entire keynote has grown steadily clearer, louder, and sweeter. Not a single vibration of its melodious strings has been lost. I have more and more clearly elucidated my subject as year after year has flown, until now its claims may not be misunderstood. Was Newton capable of satisfactorily stating the laws of gravitation when first he discovered that ponderous principle? Much less could I, at first, formulate and express the infinite Principle and the divine laws of which God gave me the first faint gleam in my hour of physical agony and mental illumination. All true Christian Scientists realize, to some extent, my early honest struggles. I was not poor till I renounced my old faith, and declined to write on any other subject. After I had left all to follow Christ, I was poor in this world's wealth for several years, but was growing rich in God's bestowals.

I climbed to the sun-crowned heights of Christian Science through the illumined truths of Holy Writ, and by precept and example. It required a deep study of the Scriptures, in the words of St. Paul, "a life hid with Christ in God." And I am still kneeling at the feet of Christ.

The sword is not used in defense of myself, for the "new tongue" is not yet generally understood, but my life as well as teaching have carried conviction to students and to the sick that God is doing the work whereof I speak. When reviled and persecuted, I revile not again; but wait on the ages to illumine His pages.

In the chapter on "Fruitage," which appears in the 226th edition of my work *Science and Health,* may be seen an inkling of the fruit of my labors.

I look for no general comprehension of scientific metaphysical propositions at present: they must seem abstract to minds not touched by this divine fire. But the obvious fact is that all who do understand Christian Science are invincible in their admiration of its Christlike character, and demonstrate its truth, utility, and practicability every day. Christian Science lays the axe at the root of the tree; it unfolds theodicy, which indicates the harmony of all emanating from the divine Mind; and the liability to err of any supposed opposite power—evil, occultism, animal magnetism, hypnotism.

Dr. Asa G. Eddy Attacked

A recent resurrection of the buried past compels me to repeat the following.

In 1878, the Court in Boston unearthed a foul conspiracy against the fair name of my husband.[88] The press had sent throughout our land and abroad the statement that Dr. Asa G. Eddy had been arrested for conspiracy to murder one Daniel H. Spofford. At the same time this so-called murdered man was well and hidden away in Boston. Rev. Russell Conwell, D.D., of Philadelphia, Pennsylvania—at that time a prominent attorney in Boston—was Mr. Eddy's counsel. The principal witness against him testified in court that Mr. Eddy gave him money and employed him to kill Spofford; afterward said witness confessed that he lied, and said he never saw Mr. Eddy until he saw him in court.

Mr. Eddy was Daniel H. Spofford's friend, and I his benefactor. He had helped Spofford, given him gratuitous use of his office, its furniture, and so forth. I am glad to say that I now believe Mr. Spofford was wronged, and unwittingly drawn by his enemies into that conspiracy. Forever to make plain the diabolism of this infamous

Daniel H. Spofford (1842–1924). An early student of Christian Science, Daniel Spofford ran the Christian Scientist Publishing Company in 1876 at the request of Mary Baker Eddy. The next year, he broke with Eddy and Christian Science. From a visiting card in Eddy's photograph album.

proceeding, I append these extracts from the chapter on "Demonology" in my third edition of *Science and Health*.

> The case was called in the Municipal Court, 1878. The principal witnesses for the prosecution were convicts and inmates of houses of ill-fame in Boston. The detectives put the defendants into court, mainly relying on the testimony of one S[argent], whose testimony was elaborate in detail.
>
> The principal point of his statement was that he met Dr. Eddy and Arens on a railroad track in East Cambridge, on the 17th of August, 1878, at 5:30 p.m., to arrange for putting D. S[pofford] out of the way. He said he was certain of the time, having noted it by a seizure on a rum-shop made at 5:30 on that day. Said he had placed the witness C[ollier] in a freight car to hear whatever conversation might occur, so that his testimony should confirm his own. He further said he was paid money by E. J. Arens, in Boston, and by Dr. Eddy, at his house in Lynn.

The following affidavit, which was made before a justice in Taunton, Massachusetts, on the 17th of December, 1878, makes plain this wicked conspiracy:

> I, George A. Collier, do on oath depose and say of my own free will, and in order to expose the man who has tried to injure Dr. Asa G. Eddy and E. J. Arens, that S[argent] did induce me, by great persuasion, to go with him to East Cambridge, from Boston, on or about the 7th day of November last, the day of the hearing in the Municipal Court of Boston in the case of Dr. Asa G. Eddy and E. J. Arens for attempting to hire said S[argent] to kill one D. S[pofford], and that he showed me the place and the cars that he was going to swear to, and told me what to say in court, and made me repeat the story until I

knew it well, so that I could tell the same story that he would; and there was not one word of truth in it all. I never heard a conversation in East Cambridge between said Eddy and Arens and S[argent], or saw them pay, or offer to pay, S[argent]any money.

George A. Collier.

The following affidavit is from one of the old and much respected citizens of Lynn:

Lynn
May 12, 1881

Detective P[inkham] stated in court, or before the grand Jury (I think), that Mr.[Arens] and Dr. Eddy were with him at No. 8 Broad St. on a certain day, and paid him some money, while I can state that they were both at 71½ Market St., Lynn, all the afternoon of that day, and at the precise time testified to by said P[inkham] that he was with them at No. 8 Broad St. Mr. P[inkham] has said to me that the testimonies of all the parties in the case were perjuries.

David Austin

Personally appeared before me the above-named David Austin, and acknowledged this to be his free act and deed.

H. L. Bancroft, Notary Public

The editors of leading newspapers, who entertained no purpose to injure the cause of Christian healing, made honorable amends for the articles they had published. The following is taken from the *Boston Evening Transcript*, Feb. 22nd, 1879:

THAT CONSPIRACY

The case brought by D. S[pofford] last October against Dr. Eddy and E. J. Arens, of Lynn, has been nol pros'd. The confession under oath of one of the real conspirators, that he was employed to testify falsely, is supported by other direct evidence. Dr. Eddy was president of the association that expelled Daniel Spofford. He, Dr. Eddy, is a member of the Baptist Church, and bears an excellent character. Mrs. Glover Eddy's most intimate acquaintances say her life and teachings are of the highest character.

May the hour be not distant when the kindling rays of divine Love shall lift the long night of ignorance, subtlety, and crime, flooding the world with light, and establishing universal brotherhood, "Peace on earth and good will to man!"

The state removed the detectives who arrested my husband, and the other two principal witnesses were taken to jail on previous charges.

A public dinner was tendered to Dr. Asa G. Eddy, and everything possible was done to make amends for the unjust prosecution. A law relating to libel was also immediately passed to prevent the recurrence of similar outrages.

Soon after we were settled in our new home on Columbus Avenue, Boston, and had established the Massachusetts Metaphysical College, I suggested to my husband that he take a brief respite from his labors, and shall never forget his answer: "Mary, I cannot leave you alone with all these burdens upon you; and then, to be away from you would be akin to death."

My legal counsel, at the time I employed them, were able and honorable members of the bar; only one has lost his high standing, and this about eight years after I left Boston and stopped employing him.

Infringement of
Science and Health

No bygone history of the dead would ever be reproduced by me were it not drawn out by falsehoods published concerning it.

A decision of the United States Circuit Court at Boston affords further evidence upon this subject. I quote from an article in the *Christian Science Sentinel* of February 16, 1899. The article is entitled, "Infringement of *Science and Health,* etc. The Decision of the United States Circuit Court."

This decision was based upon a proceeding instituted by Mrs. Eddy against one Edward J. Arens, to restrain him from publishing a pamphlet printed and issued by him, which, for the most part, contained matter pirated from the works of Mrs. Mary Baker G. Eddy. Some time later, the said Arens having published another pamphlet differing a little from the first one, the bill was amended to include this second piracy. Arens, in his answer, alleged that the copyrighted works of Mrs. Eddy were not original with her, but had been copied by her, or by her direction, from manuscript originally composed by Dr. P. P. Quimby.

The time for taking testimony on the part of the defendant, Arens, having nearly expired, he

Edward J. Arens. This early follower of Christian Science tried to assist Mary Baker Eddy by involving her in ill-considered and unsuccessful lawsuits. Later, after breaking with her, he published pamphlets plagiarizing her writings. From a visiting card in Eddy's photograph album.

gave notice, through his counsel, that he should not put in any testimony, and a stipulation for a judgement and decree in favor of Mrs. Eddy was drawn up and signed by his counsel. [*Miscellaneous Writings,* page 381, referring to the failure on the part of defendant Arens' counsel to introduce proof in support of his answer, says: Mrs. Eddy requested her lawyer to inquire of defendant's counsel why he did not present evidence to support his claim that Dr. Quimby was the author of her writings? Accordingly, her counsel asked the defendant's counsel this question, and he replied, in substance, "There is no evidence to present."] Upon the filing of this stipulation, the following decree was made by the Court.

CIRCUIT COURT OF THE UNITED STATES

District of Massachusetts
Decree for Perpetual Injunction

Sept. 24, 1883. It is ordered, adjudged, and decreed as follows: that the copyright heretofore obtained by the complainant under the name of Mary Baker Glover, upon the book entitled *The Science of Man,* etc., and the copyright upon the book entitled *Science and Health,* Vol. 2, by Mary Baker Glover Eddy, whereby there was secured good and valid copyrights, that the said defendant has infringed the said copyrights, and upon the exclusive rights of the complainant under the same, by publication, sale and distribution of the works *The Understanding of Christianity or God,* etc., and *Christianity, or the Understanding of God,* etc., by Edward J. Arens.

And it is further ordered, adjudged and decreed, that a perpetual injunction be issued against the defendant according to the prayer of the bill.

And it is further ordered, etc., that the complainant recover of the defendant her cost of suit taxed at ($113.09) one hundred and thirteen and 9/100 dollars.

By the Court,
Alex. H. Trowbridge
Deputy Clerk

And upon such decree the following injunction was issued and served upon E. J. Arens:

UNITED STATES OF AMERICA
Massachusetts District, ss.
The President of the United States of America to
E. J. Arens, of Boston, in the
State of Massachusetts,
Your Agents and Servants send Greeting
Whereas—

Mary B. G. Eddy, of said Boston, has exhibited her Bill of Complaint before the Justice of our Circuit Court of the United States for the First Circuit, begun and holden at Boston, within and for the District of Massachusetts, on the fifteenth day of May, A.D. 1883, against you, the said

Edward J. Arens,

praying to be relieved touching the matters therein complained of; and whereas, by an Order from said Court, made on the twenty-fourth day of September, A.D. 1883, it was ordered that a Writ of Injunction issue, under seal of the said Court, to restrain you, and each and every of you, from doing all the matters and things, from the doing of which you are prayed to be restrained in said Bill, according in full with the prayer of said Bill.

Science and Health.

A Book of about Five Hundred Pages.

By MARY BAKER GLOVER,

OF NEW HAMPSHIRE.

A Metaphysical Treatise showing how Disease is Caused and Cured
by MIND instead of Matter.

READ IT !

"For that which had not been told them shall they see; and that
which they had not heard shall they consider."

Comments and Quotations.

EXTRACTS FROM LETTERS.

"Your remarkable volume, 'Science and Health,' I have read with
profound interest. The sound truths you announce, sustained by facts of
the immortal life, give to your work the seal of inspiration — reaffirm in
modern phrase the Christian revelations."—*A. Bronson Alcott.*

"We hope you will be spared to educate many more pupils, that thereby mankind shall be blessed."—*Hon. B. F. Atkinson.*

"We have read *Science and Health* and the reviews. Your book is
not issued at a date most favorable to its reception, it is in advance of
the period, but is needed all the more for this. To conclude this Metaphysical treatise is far from scientific, the propositions of which are logical, many of the facts fulfilled before our eyes, the candid evidence

Advertising circular for the first edition of *Science and Health*. Though the book was
published in 1875, this advertisement probably dates from the following year.

We, therefore, in consideration thereof, enjoin and command you, each and every of you that from, and immediately after the receipt and notice of this, our Writ, by you, or any of you, you shall not, directly or indirectly, print, publish, sell, give away, distribute, or in any way or manner dispose of a certain work or book entitled *The Understanding of Christianity or God,* etc., by Edward J. Arens; or a certain work or book entitled *Christianity, or the Understanding of God,* etc., by Edward J. Arens; which said books are copies from, and infringements of the copyrighted works of the complainant, as set forth in Bill of Complaint in this cause. Whereof you are not to fail, on pain of ten thousand dollars, to be levied on your and each of your goods, chattels, lands and tenements, to our use.

Witness:

The Honorable Morrison R. Waite, at Boston, this twenty-seventh day of September, in the year of our Lord, one thousand eight hundred and eighty-three.

Alex. H. Trowbridge

Deputy Clerk

UNITED STATES OF AMERICA

Massachusetts District, ss.

Boston

Oct. 4, 1883

I hereby acknowledge personal service of within injunction.

Edward J. Arens

Concerning this decree the editor of *The Christian Science Journal* said:

It seems scarcely necessary to add, that Mr. Arens's defense, as set forth in his answer, having been that the works, the copyright of which he infringed, were not original with Mrs. Eddy, he would, had it been possible, have produced the proof necessary to support his answer. It is evident this defense was vital in the case, as he apparently had no other. The fact that he failed to produce his proof is conclusive evidence that no such proof existed.

No honest or disinterested person, in the face of this record, would undertake to falsify the record by insisting that Mrs. Eddy's works were plagiarized from Dr. Quimby's writings. The absurdity, as well as the utter falsity of this claim, are at once apparent. Let us hope that, as a mere matter of self-respect, if for no other reason, the persons now lending themselves to the circulation of the falsehood will awaken to their error, and see that they are merely stultifying themselves.

Never to my knowledge did I prosecute Spofford for mental malpractice. Mr. Arens had been heard to say Spofford ought to be prosecuted for mental malpractice on Miss Brown, and through proceedings unknown to me, he may have used my name in some way without my authority. As, for example, on another occasion Arens asked me for a note of $1,000 that a student had given me and which I had never tried to collect. He said if I would give it to him, he would collect it without legal proceedings; that he was poor, and that the student was able to pay it. So, out of kindness I gave him the note, on the condition that he should not involve me in the matter, or use my name. He promised not to use it in any way. Shortly afterwards, however, a suit was brought in my name against said debtor by said Arens.

Christian Science
versus Spiritualism

It would seem like supererogation to say that I never was a spiritualist or medium, and never gave a séance. But I do declare this emphatically. I did investigate this subject, before my discovery of Christian Science, to learn its phenomena, cause, and effect. As a result of this research I abandoned the subject.

About 1862 I delivered a lecture on spiritualism in the City Hall at Portland, Maine, and it was said by hundreds present to have been the most convincing argument they ever listened to against spiritualism. I never mesmerized a person to my knowledge—am ignorant of how it can be done—and it astounds me more than most sins, to conceive of its being done.

It was a common thing then, if a person manifested mentally aught outré, for spiritualists forthwith to declare, such a one is a spiritualist, or a medium controlled by spirits. Rev. Henry Ward Beecher, Theodore Parker, and the poet Whittier, were said to be under spirit control.

Honest thinkers say that in open, honest explanation of spiritualism, as mental phenomena, in no wise connected with the departed, I have accomplished more than any other person on earth. Hence the shafts aimed at me on this subject. Shall the disciple murmur who drinks of the cup of his Lord; or shall the humblest follower of Christ think to escape the fiery exalting ordeal of sin's revenge on its destroyer?

The Mother Church

In 1882 we moved from Lynn to 569 Columbus Avenue, Boston, Massachusetts. Our cause grew so rapidly in that city a church edifice was projected. To this end I purchased and gave to the church the lot of land on which stands The First Church of Christ, Scientist, in Boston. The following letter from the Directors of this church gives the facts concerning this transaction:

Owing to a loss of about $4,000 contributed towards paying for the land on which the church edifice was to be erected, Mrs. Eddy, as usual, came to the rescue of her church and purchased the mortgage on the lot of land on the corner of Falmouth and Caledonia (now Norway) streets in Boston, paying therefore the sum of $4,963.50 and interest, through her counsel.

After the mortgage had expired and the note given therewith became due, legal proceedings were instituted by her counsel, advertising the property in the Boston newspapers & c., thus giving opportunity for those who had previously negotiated for the property to redeem the land by paying the amount due on the mortgage and thereby becoming owners of the land. But no one offered Mrs. Eddy the price she had paid for it, nor to take the property off her hands, so the mortgage was foreclosed and the land legally conveyed, with a clear title to Mrs. Eddy, by her counsel.

After the above transaction Mrs. Eddy conveyed the lot to trustees for the purpose of having a church building erected thereon. On receiving the deed, the trustees had a plan drawn for a church building that would seat about 775 people; declaring it to be their intention to build a publishing house on the remainder of the land in connection with the church. Mrs. Eddy objected to this on the ground that such was not the intention of the deed, and through her counsel, Streeter & Walker, of Concord, N.H., she had the land deeded back to her, and conveyed it to another Board of Trustees who were to be known as "The Christian Science Board of Directors" (a copy of this deed is published in the *Church Manual*). To prevent all future difficulty about this church property, her counsel, Reuben E. Walker (now associate Judge of the Supreme Court of New Hampshire), advised her to give a trust deed conveying a beneficiary use of the land to her church, The First Church of Christ, Scientist, in Boston, in order to make it safe for her church; she has derived no personal advantage from it whatever. Neither she nor her heirs or assigns can legally mortgage, rent, remove, or sell this church build-

The original edifice of The Mother Church, dedicated in 1895. The building was erected in Boston's Back Bay, at the convergence of Norway and Falmouth Street.

ing. In her deed of the church lot to the Directors of this church she retains only this privilege; namely, in case the church should use this edifice for other purposes than a house of worship, she could deed it to other parties for the proper uses of a church of our denomination.

Mrs. Eddy's transaction in redeeming the mortgage on the land gave those who had previously contributed toward purchasing the land opportunity to recover it beneficially and build a church on it. No one person contributed $7,000, or even one-half this sum to the church fund, for land or the church building, except Mrs. Josephine C. Otterson, deceased, of Brooklyn, New York. The balance due on the mortgage at the time it was purchased was $4,963.50 and interest; only a little over $5,000 had been paid altogether before the mortgage expired, and was foreclosed.

After the building was completed, the church, through the Christian Science Board of Directors and their agents, presented the church edifice to Mrs. Eddy, accompanying the gift with a large gold scroll on which the presentation was engraved.

Mrs. Eddy declined to receive the gift of the church edifice, any remuneration for her trouble and expense in redeeming the land, or even a salary from her church. When the church edifice was being built, by her own personal effort she raised over $40,000 and contributed it toward the building fund. We fail to see anything in this entire transaction of the Reverend Mrs. Eddy's which can be misconstrued; and we do see a benevolence that characterizes her entire life.

The Christian Science Board of Directors
Ira O. Knapp
William B. Johnson, Clerk
Joseph Armstrong
Stephen A. Chase, Treasurer
Boston, Mass.
Jan. 27, 1902

Presentation of the Church Edifice

Boston
March 19, 1895

To the Reverend Mary Baker G. Eddy, our beloved teacher and leader:

We are happy to announce to you the completion of The First Church of Christ, Scientist, in Boston.

In behalf of your loving students, and all contributors wherever they may be, we hereby present this church to you as a testimonial of love and gratitude for your labors and loving sacrifice, as the discoverer and founder of Christian Science, and the author of its textbook *Science and Health with Key to the Scriptures.*

We therefore respectfully extend to you the invitation to become the permanent pastor of this church, in connection with the Bible and the Book alluded to above, which you have already ordained as our pastor. And we most cordially invite you to be present and take charge of any services that may be held therein. We especially desire you to be present on the twenty-fourth day of March, eighteen hundred and ninety-five, to accept this offering, with our humble benediction.

Lovingly Yours,

The Christian Science Board of Directors
Ira O. Knapp
William B. Johnson
Joseph Armstrong
Stephen A. Chase

The Christian Science Board of Directors, standing on the steps of The Mother Church, in about 1895. Left to right: Ira O. Knapp, William B. Johnson, Joseph Armstrong, and Stephen A. Chase.

To this tender letter from the Board of Directors, I replied:

Beloved Directors and Brethren:

For your costly offering, and kind call again to the pastorate of The First Church of Christ, Scientist, in Boston, accept my profound thanks. But permit me respectfully to decline their acceptance, while I fully appreciate your kind intentions. If it will comfort you in the least, make me your Pastor Emeritus, nominally. Through my book, your textbook, I already speak to you each Sunday. You ask too much when asking me to accept your grand church edifice. I have more of earth now than I desire, and less of heaven; so pardon my refusal of that be-quest. More effectual than the forum are our states of mind, to bless mankind. This my wish stops not with my pen—God give you grace. As our church's tall tower detains the sun, so may luminous lines from your lives linger, a legacy to our race.[89]

Mary Baker G. Eddy
March 25, 1895

THE CHRISTIAN SCIENCE BOARD OF DIRECTORS OF THE FIRST CHURCH OF CHRIST, SCIENTIST

Falmouth and Norway Sts.,
Boston, Mass.
March 21st, 1895

To the Reverend Mary Baker G. Eddy
Pleasant View
Concord, N.H.

Dear Mother:

At a regular meeting of The Christian Science Board of Directors, held this day, you were unanimously appointed Pastor Emeritus of The Mother Church, The First Church of Christ, Scientist, in Boston, Mass., and we pray you to accept this office at our hands.

The Christian Science Board of Directors
Edward P. Bates, Secretary

The First Church of Christ, Scientist, in Boston has about 22,000 communicants in January, 1902. While these people, and a million others of this denomination, reassure the public as to the faith, religion, and the life of their Leader—and the officers of my church as to her business veracity, if forsooth they are satisfied, whose business is it to complain?

Offices at 95 Falmouth Street, home for The Christian Science Publishing Society and other publishing activities of The First Church of Christ, Scientist, 1895–1903. These activities expanded to adjacent buildings at 97 and 99 Falmouth. The buildings were demolished to make way for the Extension of The Mother Church.

I exercise no power over my church, apart from exacting compliance with its By-Laws, which the church adopts. I decline to receive even a salary. Human deification or worship I abjure, as all know who have a true knowledge of me. The hundreds of thousands who adhere to me do so simply from love.

The Christian Science Publishing Society

I had given my *Christian Science Journal* to the National Christian Scientist Association, when, about 1889, said Association by a unanimous vote of its members authorized that the copyright of *The Christian Science Journal* and the property connected therewith be conveyed to me. Shortly afterwards I caused a trust deed to be executed, by which I conveyed this entire property to my church, The First Church of Christ, Scientist, in Boston. Also I selected a Board of Trustees that should manage the business of The Christian Science Publishing Society, specifying that all net profits accruing from said business should be paid to my church. I retained no personal financial benefit from this property save the free use of rooms in the Christian Science Publishing House, wherein to publish and sell my books.

In making this transfer from the members of the The Christian Science Publishing Society to the new Board of Trustees, I gave to each of the three members of this Society out of my own private funds $2,000. By this transaction I gave to The Mother Church what had legally become my personal property, a sum valued at about $50,000. Also I paid from my private funds the entire cost of the transfer.

1

8

Footprints Fadeless

The Massachusetts Metaphysical College

MASSACHUSETTS
Metaphysical College.

This institution, chartered by the Commonwealth of Massachusetts in 1881, receives both male and female students.

It gives ample instruction in every scientific method of medicine.

It meets the demand of the age for something higher than physic or drugging to restore to the race hope and health.

Metaphysics are taught on a purely practical basis, to aid the developement of mind, and to impart the understanding of the power and resources of the mind that promote and restore health and spiritually elevate man.

Students can at any time enter their names for the Collegiate course, and will be given two weeks' notice of when the Term commences. Tuition $300. Reduction to indigent students.

Address for further particulars,

REV. M. B. G. EDDY, PRES'T.
571 Columbus Ave., Boston, Mass.

TAKE NOTICE.

ONLY those who can show credentials to that effect, have been my students.

MARY BAKER G. EDDY, President.

Advertisement for the Massachusetts Metaphysical College. This notice appeared in an early issue of the *Journal of Christian Science*.

This college was incorporated under the laws of Massachusetts January 31, 1881. There was a pause in its functions during my absence and revision of *Science and Health,* but the charter was not surrendered—and the laws of Massachusetts have found no fault with my manner of conducting this college *twenty-one years.* My Christian Scientists Home was a charitable institute; the students received their board and tuition free.

My Secretary's Letter

In 1881, I entered the Rev. Mary Baker G. Eddy's class in Christian Science at Lynn, Mass. I was a widower, my wife having passed away in 1872. Since then I have never married. For fifteen years previous to becoming a Christian Scientist, I was an active member of the Congregational Church.

During class instruction, I boarded with Dr. Asa G. Eddy and Mrs. Eddy, at their home in Lynn, and it was a *happy home*. In August, 1882, I entered Mrs. Eddy's employ as bookkeeper and secretary at the Massachusetts Metaphysical College, in Boston, and have lived in her family continuously since then. During these twenty years, I have seen her work unselfishly, educating students to fill important posts in our Cause. In some few instances her labors to help students have been met not only with her disappointment at their failures, but with their persistent envy and falsehood.

Although her rebuke is strong, yet she is most tender towards all striving to do right. Her patience under wrong and injustice is proverbial. Her devout life, her moral and spiritual influence are unimpeachable and they are strong incentives to students who come under her benign teachings.

Mrs. Eddy gives herself no respite from care and declines to receive any salary for all her manifold services. Her only source of revenue is from the sales of her books, and the interest accruing from her savings. As her bookkeeper I know that she gives away annually a large sum in private charities. These gifts have in some years amounted to $80,000. She never speculates in stock; owns neither railroad, corporation, or mining stock, and has no financial interest in souvenir spoons! I have heard her say, "I might have been a millionaire, but I would never be that while so many people are poor."

I name this instance of her patience: I knew a person who served her as steward in Boston. She knew that person was honest. He took the

Calvin A. Frye, personal secretary to Mary Baker Eddy, with stacks of work on his desk at Pleasant View. It is possible that Calvin Frye took this photograph himself by using a remote shutter release (note the position of his left hand). From his own photograph album.

money from her with orders to pay the grocer and butcher monthly. After three months, neither one having received any payment on his bills, both made it known to Mrs. Eddy. She told them she had given the money monthly to her employee to pay them. The latter was then called to account. He said he had received the money from Mrs. Eddy, but knew not what had become of it. She then sadly recognized the cause, saw he was the victim of mental malicious malpractice, rebuked him sternly and pointed out the consequences of his yielding to this sin. The grocer and butcher advised Mrs. Eddy not to have too much charity, they thought it was unreasonable. She settled the matter by paying their bills, and nothing further was said on the subject. She believed that that student, left to himself, was strictly honest. He offered to refund the missing money to her, but her sympathy with his situation made her refuse it. It were needless to add this student was saved from becoming again the victim of this infernal spell.

Mrs. Eddy is most conscientious in her business transactions; I have seen her often wrong herself (in a business way) to help another. Honesty is indelibly stamped upon every act of hers. Her unselfishness, solid trust in God, and her patience with sinners often astonish me.

More than once she has received anonymous letters containing threats to kill her, and unimpeachable people have informed her of the attempt of mental malpractitioners to kill her.

I have learned in Christian Science that it is impossible to heal the sick, and to do the good that Mrs. Eddy is continually doing, and at the same time, to mentally possess the power to make folks sick, or to harm them. While it can be shown that some of her accusers teach people to mentally murder folks, and they themselves commit this crime. These folks are trying to make it appear that Mrs. Eddy is as wicked as they are, but they cannot. Twenty years of observation have convinced me that her character can bear all the strain that can be put on it, and then remain a model for the rest of us. I sometimes have thought that her reproof and instruction were more than I could bear, but I stood it, and am all the better for it.

For twenty years I have kept account of the classes that Mrs. Eddy has taught. During this time she never taught a class without having in it some members to whom she gave their tuition. Sometimes she had sixteen charity students in one class. She has accepted applicants for her class without payment, and rejected others offering full tuition. I never knew her to countenance sin in any form, much less to teach any one to mentally malpractice—something that she does not know how to teach, or to practice herself; but she can perceive its effects sooner than others. I also know that no person can harm another while adhering to the theory and practice that she teaches.

For many years she did all the pioneer work for the cause of Christian Science, and paid the expenses therefore almost entirely from her own funds, and there was no attempt to challenge her grand life. Out of five thousand students the average is less than one per cent of the entire number who do not love and reverence her, and a million people thank God for giving her to the world.

Calvin A. Frye
Pleasant View
Concord, N.H.
Jan. 25, 1902

Marriage Not Prohibited

Christian Science does not prohibit marriage; it leaves this act as optional with the individual, as it is in any religious denomination. I never advise a person not to marry, except I see in that person, or in the circumstances, an existing unfitness for this relation.

I leave the subject of marriage and progeny, in my private teachings, just as they are found in my published works, and the chapter on "Marriage," in *Science and Health,* which all approve. I advise no separation between husband and wife if by any right means it can be avoided; but recommend that they remain together, trust God's providence, and wait on it.

I copy from *Science and Health with Key to the Scriptures,* 204th edition, the following: This has been in our textbook ever since its 50th edition.

> Separation never should take place: and it never would, if the husband and wife were genuine Christian Scientists. Science inevitably lifts one's being higher in the scale of harmony and happiness.

Mental Malpractice

I would sooner permit a doctor infected with smallpox to attend me than be treated mentally by a practitioner who obeys not the Golden Rule according to Christ's requirements. I thoroughly denounce all mental practice that is unchristian; and had been healing and teaching in Christian Science seven years before I knew of mental malpractice.

A thief makes no haste to acknowledge stealing, nor a murderer to confess his crime. Neither does the mental malpractitioner report himself, nor expose his method. Those persons who write to editors of newspapers that "Mrs. Eddy is sick," "She is palsied," or "She is dead," when daily I am performing laborious functions that most women would think impossible; we may suspect of being mental malpractitioners, since by these public declarations, they may aim to strengthen their private endeavors. I name the above only as a fair illustration of silly fabrications.

The moral and spiritual facts of being are whispered into thought through Christian Science, and thus the patient is healed by Truth, after the manner of prayer. Other methods material, limited to drugs, or subject to evil communications, have none of the advantages of Truth or Christian mental healing.

For the last decade the mental malpractice of some disloyal students, together with their public adverse declarations, have been continually aimed at me, while I am praying daily, "God bless my enemies, and save them from sin." Christian Science can harm no one; but it can, does, help the sinner and the sick outward, onward, upward. I never practised or taught a student to practise contrary to the Scripture and the laws of our land. To this fact every loyal student will testify.

When first my students came to me to know how they could defend themselves and their patients against the attacks of mental malpractitioners, we knew it was wrong to attack any one, but thought it right to defend our own lives, and the lives of others. But not long thereafter we put up the sword, and anchored our trust alone in God to deliver us from our enemies.

After the death of my husband, Dr. Eddy, I sent for one of the mental malpractitioners to come and look on his calm, dear face. The

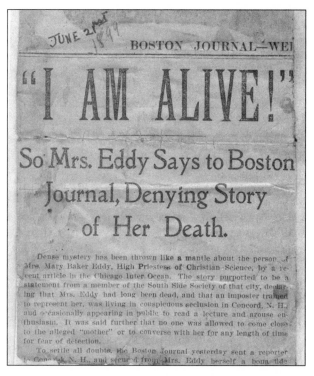

JUNE 21st 1899

BOSTON JOURNAL—WEI

"I AM ALIVE!"

So Mrs. Eddy Says to Boston Journal, Denying Story of Her Death.

Dense mystery has been thrown like a mantle about the person of Mrs. Mary Baker Eddy, High Priestess of Christian Science, by a recent article in the Chicago Inter Ocean. The story purported to be a statement from a member of the South Side Society of that city, declaring that Mrs. Eddy had long been dead, and that an imposter trained to represent her, was living in conspicuous seclusion in Concord, N. H., and occasionally appearing in public to read a lecture and arouse enthusiasm. It was said further that no one was allowed to come close to the alleged "mother" or to converse with her for any length of time for fear of detection.

To settle all doubts, the Boston Journal yesterday sent a reporter to Concord, N. H., and secured from Mrs. Eddy herself a bona fide

Newspaper article, *Boston Journal*, June 21, 1899. With both charm and forcefulness, Mary Baker Eddy refuted reports of her death in this interview.

messenger, who stood at the door and delivered my request, said that on hearing it, he grew deadly pale and clutched at the door to stand. He never came.

At another time a good man whose life I had been the means of saving, wrote to me that a large number of mental malpractitioners had appointed a day on which to unite in their mental process to kill me. On the day mentioned I committed my way unto God and He directed my path.

To-day every loyal Christian Scientist's remedy against mental malicious attacks is to overcome evil with good—to watch, work, pray.

The little that I know of the meaning of the word "agamogenesis"[90] is gathered from lexicons, and discredited by me as properly belonging or applied to the human species. One instance of mental aberration came to my knowledge, which I named to my students as a startling phenomenon of insanity: A young lady of good character, and the patient of a Christian Scientist, had the symptoms and appearance of maternity. From what she assured her healer, the latter believed in her integrity of conduct, and treated her for hallucination—for she had previously shown symptoms of incipient insanity—when all the symptoms of pregnancy disappeared. I have named this exceptional case to my students only as a new and startling phenomenon of insanity, and the so-called power of misguided belief. I believe the Scripture: "All things were made by Him." The human, the animal, vegetable, or mineral has no propagating power. God, good, made all and it was *good*.

The Late Governor
Moody Currier's Letter

The late Governor Moody Currier of New Hampshire was a great and good man—highly esteemed for his executive ability as chief magistrate of the state, and a scholar—wrote as follows. He was not a Christian Scientist.

Manchester, N.H.
August 17, 1895

My dear Mrs. Eddy:

Some days since I had the pleasure of receiving by express two nice volumes, containing your card, showing that I am indebted to you for the very welcome present for which I most heartily thank you. From a hasty examination I am sure I shall receive much satisfaction in their further perusal and study.

It gives me great pleasure to find your system so free from mystical creeds and theological dogmas. Every theory of philosophy or religion in order to stand the scientific criticism of the present day must be founded upon the eternal laws of God. The original method of your teachings reminds me very forcibly of the characteristic manner of your lamented brother, Albert, who thoroughly despised every appearance of sham and pretence in pretended teachers of mankind.

I wish to congratulate you upon the broad and independent foundation on which you are now building your great work and trust that your fame and renown may last as long as the principles you teach.

Very sincerely yours,

Moody Currier

A Matter of Hearts

In letters to students whom I was struggling to reform, I have written, "You would tear my heart out and trample on it." By slight changes such as certain reporters have made in my newspaper articles, that sentence could easily be made to read falsely. If I must wound any heart, I would prefer to have it my own rather than another's. Both my private and public life have proven this simple fact. Stern and uncompromising in rebuking sin I am, but ill temper or revenge I consider weak and wicked, defeating itself. People who know me will say, whether I lose temper under wrong or falsehood, I find a better way out of it.

When I legally adopted Ebenezer J. Foster Eddy,[91] M.D., C.S.D.,[92] in Boston, Massachusetts, he was a bachelor, his mother was dead, and his father was married to a second wife. There is no quarrel between us. The following letter I received from him last October. In the family circle he is known as "Benny."

My most blessed Mother:

Your letter came in due time, and it was so sweet and precious, just like you. And to think you took so much of your valuable time to write all of which I appreciate and thank you for it very much.

Please tell Mr. Frye the trunk came all right, and thank him. I had forgotten

Ebenezer J. Foster Eddy (1847–1930). In 1888 Mary Baker Eddy adopted Ebenezer Foster, a student of Christian Science who had formerly studied homeopathic medicine. She broke all ties with him in 1897. Cabinet card photograph.

what was in the trunk. He did not put my music in, but that does not matter very much.

There is no one under the canopy of heaven that I should be so delighted to see as you; but I willingly forego any personal pleasure, if it will spare you the least in any way. Believe me when I say nothing whatsoever shall diminish the pure love and esteem I have for you, and I shall try to hold myself in readiness to come to you whenever you shall deem it best.

With lots of love from your

Benny
Waterbury, Vt.
Oct. 22, 1901

No photographs of me are extant that were not made until after I was in the sixties and later; and the negatives for the earliest of these were made in 1886.

Wayside Hints

Rev. Mr. Wiggin's[93] "Wayside Hints," with my comments, appeared in some of the early nos. of *The Christian Science Journal.* I never preached a sermon of his, or the sermon of any person excepting my own. At one time he gave me a subject and asked me for the explanation. I chose a text in reference thereto, wrote his inquiries on a slip of paper, and thought I placed them in my Bible. When opening to the chapter selected for Sunday service, I missed my notes and found I had failed to take them with me. However, I preached from my text; at the

close of the service Mr. Wiggin extended to me his congratulations, said
my explanation of the points alluded
to was perfectly satisfactory. I then
told him what had happened.

Mr. Wiggin had been a Unitarian
clergyman; he was a grand man and
often attended my church. For a short
time he edited *The Christian Science
Journal,* and was proofreader for some
of my writings.

After writing my scriptural exege-
sis of the spiritual and material creations, without knowledge of two
independent documentary accounts of
Creation—namely the Elohistic and
the Jehovistic—Mr. Wiggin brought
to me a pamphlet treating the subject.
He said, "Did you not know of this
before writing *Science and Health?*" I
replied, "No." He was amazed at this,
became interested, and afterwards read my book.

The Reverend James Henry Wiggin (1836–
1900). Mary Baker Eddy employed Wiggin from
time to time as a kind of editorial consultant.
Cabinet card photograph.

The Rev. Dr. Peabody, Chaplain of Harvard, and other clergymen, at
my request, used to preach for me in my absence.

Christic, One and Divine

It would seem that I had reiterated sufficiently my views on Christ to have them well known. In my church tenets are these words: "We acknowledge *one* Christ." I regard Christ as divine, and myself as a human being seeking Christ.

A telegram to the *New York Herald*,[94] printed in that newspaper February 6, 1895, contained in substance the following:

Concord, N.H.
February 1, 1895

A despatch is handed to me, calling for an interview to answer for myself, "Am I the second Christ?"

Even the question shocks me. What I am is for God to declare in His infinite mercy. I claim nothing more than to be the Discoverer and Founder of Christian Science—the blessing this is to mankind, eternity enfolds.

My books and teachings maintain but one conclusion and statement of the Christ; also the fable and profanity of deifying mortals.

There never was, is not, and never can be but one God, one Christ, one Jesus of Nazareth. Whoever in any age expresses most of the spirit of Truth and Love, the divine Principle of God's man, has most of the spirit of Christ, most of that Mind which was in Christ Jesus.

If Christian Scientists find in my writings, teaching, and example a great degree of this spirit, they can justly declare it. But to think or speak of me as a Christ, they do not, and it were sacrilegious, savoring more of heathenism than of my doctrine.

Mary Baker G. Eddy

In an article in the *Boston Journal,* April 11, 1899, I wrote:

> . . . all Christian Scientists deeply recognize the oneness of Jesus—that he stands alone in word and deed, the visible discoverer, founder and great Teacher of Christianity, the sandals on whose feet none may unloose.
>
> The Board of Lectureship is absolutely inclined to be, and is instructed to be, charitable towards all, hating none. The purpose of its members is to subserve the interest of mankind, and to cement the bonds of Christian brotherhood, whose every link leads upward in the chain of being. The cardinal points of Christian Science cannot be lost sight of, namely—one God, supreme, infinite, and *one* Christ Jesus.

I state my doctrines fairly, however abstract they may appear. That *Science and Health with Key to the Scriptures* was inspired seems plain to me, since I could have had no human motive for writing what was not attractive, what must cause me enemies, to leave a peaceful home, friends, and to give up my standing in society, for the toil, privation, and dishonor of a reformer.

Jesus, our great way-shower, was maligned and persecuted, but he has shown the way, and it is the victory over sin, disease, and death. It is the disappearing of the fleshly personality, and the reappearing of spiritual existence. When his demonstration is understood in Christian Science, all mankind will follow Jesus' way, and, rising above sin, disease, and death, will put off the flesh, and the error thereof, and put on the real man in the image of his Maker— even the spiritual man in Christ. This is not losing, but gaining man's eternal identity and individuality.

Rev. Irving C. Tomlinson's Letter

I present herewith a letter from a citizen of Concord, the Rev. Irving C. Tomlinson:

> I deem it a privilege as a fellow-townsman and friend of the Reverend Mary Baker G. Eddy, to refer to the high esteem in which she is held by the leading citizens of the Capital City of the Granite State.
>
> Her birthplace adjoins our municipality, her youth was spent in a neighboring community, and during the past twelve years, she has resided in this city. There are people in Concord who knew her in childhood, others were her friends in youth, and not a few of our distinguished citizens have seen her more or less frequently the past twelve years. All these people respect the honesty, integrity, and uprightness of their illustrious citizen, neighbor, and friend.
>
> She comes from an old and honored family of this Commonwealth, zealous in good works and famed for their exalted Christian character. Those in our midst who have followed her distinguished career gladly certify that she has proved worthy of her noble ancestry.
>
> Mrs. Eddy purchased and fitted up Christian Science Hall in Concord at a cost of $26,000. Because the local Christian Scientists had no suitable place in which to hold their services, and because winter was rapidly approaching, Mrs. Eddy, to hasten the enterprise, requested the builder to ask his employees, if they felt so disposed, to work upon Thanksgiving Day. The workmen accommodated her, and as token of appreciation she presented to each a five dollar gold piece, in addition to their daily wages.
>
> The urgency for haste in the completion of the structure did not prevent her exhibition of Christian kindness. At one of the busiest moments, she requested the superintendent to suspend the noise of building, lest it disturb the weekday conference of her near neighbor, the

Baptist Church. Mrs. Eddy often refers to the children's courtesy to her in the street, and her pleasure from it. She has given to our little church in Concord the sum of $100,000 for the erection of a handsome granite edifice.

Our people well know her readiness to aid the high purpose and honest endeavor of others, whether or not they be of her household of faith. The poor of our city do not forget that through her love of children two hundred pairs of shoes protect as many pairs of little feet from the winter's ice and snow.[95]

By special invitation of the officers of the New Hampshire State Fair Association, Mrs. Eddy visited their beautiful grounds in Concord on Governor's Day, 1901. She was received at the entrance by representatives of the Association, and under official escort conducted to a place of honor in front of the crowded Grand Stand, where were seated the governor and invited guests. A reception committee, consisting of the Executive Board

Irving C. Tomlinson (c. 1860–1944). Formerly a Universalist clergyman, Irving Tomlinson was associate secretary to Mary Baker Eddy from 1900 to 1902 and from August 1907 until her death in December 1910.

of the fair association, there surrounded her carriage, and stood with uncovered heads, while Mr. Moses, editor of the *Concord Daily Monitor,* in their behalf, delivered an eloquent address of welcome. This spontaneous reception reveals the patent fact that in her home city she is not only the esteemed Leader of a great religious denomination, but honored by our best people, regardless of class or creed.

Rev. Irving C. Tomlinson
Concord, N.H.
Jan. 28, 1902

Closing Words

Examples from the many editions of *Science and Health with Key to the Scriptures*. More than four hundred printings of *Science and Health* were produced during the lifetime of Mary Baker Eddy. As of 1907, numbers were no longer assigned to new editions. Eddy's final corrections appeared in the edition published a month after her passing on December 3, 1910.

Beloved brethren: Let us remember that an unwise word or deed of ours is a shovelful of earth thrown upon the grave, to which the enemies of Christ would consign Christian Science, while the rapid growth and steadfast prosperity of our denomination in the midst of persecution is God's benediction on our Christianity.

Dear Reader, I could introduce you to my witnesses across the sea, to Earl and Countess, Marquis and Marchioness, Lord and Lady; and in my native land to the best people in it, distinguished professors, poets and authors, Doctors of Divinity and Doctors of Medicine; and in my native state to New Hampshire's noblest sons and daughters, and to my attorney, General Frank S. Streeter. Also I could modestly call your attention to my church, with, I believe, the largest number of communicants of any one church in the world; and to over a million of Christian Scientists,[96] who entertain the higher hope and live the higher life—to bear testimony of me. But I chose for my witnesses the weak things of this world to confound the mighty, and call your attention to my best witness, my babe! the new-born of Truth, *Science and Health with Key to the Scriptures*—that will forever testify of itself, and its mother.

NOTES

INTRODUCTION

1. Mark Twain, *Christian Science* (New York: Oxford University Press, 1996), 102. Facsimile of the first (1907) edition. "Shameless old swindler" was a term used by Twain in a private letter in 1902. See Robert Peel, *Mary Baker Eddy: The Years of Authority* (New York: Holt, Rinehart and Winston, 1977), 446. See also Gillian Gill, *Mary Baker Eddy* (Cambridge, Mass.: Perseus Books, 1998), 336. Although Twain rejected the popular notion that Eddy had plagiarized *Science and Health* from the writings of the healer Phineas Parkhurst Quimby (see note 69), he still believed that she had not written it herself.

2. Irving C. Tomlinson, *Twelve Years with Mary Baker Eddy*, Amplified Edition (Boston: The Christian Science Publishing Society, 1996), 8.

3. Practiced by many American doctors from about the 1780s through the 1850s, heroic medicine was based on the idea that the most aggressive treatment was the best way to cure a health problem. These treatments included large doses of compounds containing substances such as lead, mercury, or opium; blood-letting; and the use of strong emetics and purgatives. Heroic medicine often did more harm than good, sometimes even causing death.

4. *Retrospection and Introspection*, 24.

5. Gill, *Mary Baker Eddy*, 324. The last numbered edition was published in 1906, though Mary Baker Eddy continued revising it until her death in 1910. The final edition, which she had authorized, appeared in 1911.

6. In 1892, Mary Baker Eddy reorganized her church and established a Board of Directors to govern it.

7. Peel, *Mary Baker Eddy: The Years of Authority*, 359.

8. Leslie Poles Hartley, *The Go-Between* (1953), prologue.

9. Gill, *Mary Baker Eddy*, 217.

10. *Science and Health*, first edition, 238.

11. *Footprints Fadeless*, 85.

12. In *Science and Health*, Eddy wrote, "The enslavement of man is not legitimate. It will cease when man enters into his heritage of freedom, his God-given dominion over the material senses. Mortals will some day assert their freedom in the name of Almighty God.", 228.

13. Colleen McDannell, *The Christian Home in Victorian America, 1840–1900* (Bloomington, Indiana: Indiana University Press, 1986), 7–8, 127–130.

14. Arthur Brisbane's interview is quoted in Gill, *Mary Baker Eddy*, 513.

15. Susan Hill Lindley, "The Ambiguous Feminism of Mary Baker Eddy," *Journal of Religion* 64 (1984), 318–331.

16. *Retrospection and Introspection*, 6–7.

17. See Catherine Wessinger, "Going Beyond and Retaining Charisma: Women's Leadership in Marginal Religions," in *Women's Leadership in Marginal Religions: Explorations Outside the Mainstream,* ed. Catherine Wessinger (Chicago: University of Illinois Press, 1993), 9.

18. Gill, *Mary Baker Eddy,* 414–415.

19. Jill Ker Conway, *When Memory Speaks: Reflections on Autobiography* (New York: Alfred A. Knopf, 1998), 87.

20. Intriguingly, Mary Baker Eddy removed these two chapters from editions of *Retrospection and Introspection* printed between 1892 and 1899, beginning the memoir instead with the chapter "Voices Not Our Own." This change called immediate attention to Eddy as a spiritual leader who was chosen even in childhood. In 1899, she decided to re-insert the genealogical chapters, though there is no real documentation as to why. Possibly she was responding to the public's desire to know more about her personal life, or she felt that those early chapters helped soften her image as a female spiritual leader.

21. Conway, *When Memory Speaks,* 107.

22. Gill, *Mary Baker Eddy,* 313.

23. *Retrospection and Introspection,* 21.

24. A 1907 affidavit as quoted in Gill, *Mary Baker Eddy,* 113. In "An Important Historical Discovery," published in the May 1983 issue of *The Christian Science Journal* (pages 284–288), Jewel Spangler Smaus

detailed the legal documents in the possession of the Glover family that further corroborated Eddy's account.

25. Gill, *Mary Baker Eddy*, 64–65.

26. *Footprints Fadeless*, 85.

27. Edwin S. Gaustad, ed., *Memoirs of the Spirit* (Grand Rapids: Eerdmans, 1999), xvi.

28. *Retrospection and Introspection*, 9.

29. Eddy addressed this discrepancy in a later publication. In 1907, in her "Reply to *McClure's Magazine*," she states that the clerk's book showed that she had joined the Congregational Church at the age of seventeen, though her "religious experience seemed to culminate at twelve years of age. Hence a mistake may have occurred as to the exact date of my first church membership." "Reply to *McClure's Magazine*," in *The First Church of Christ, Scientist, and Miscellany* (Boston: The First Church of Christ, Scientist, 1913), 311.

30. Mary Farrell Bednarowski notes the significance of the connection between Mary Baker's early theological crisis and its manifestation as physical illness. See Bednarowski, *The Religious Imagination of American Women* (Bloomington: Indiana University Press, 1999), 156.

31. *Retrospection and Introspection*, 14.

32. *Footprints Fadeless*, 108.

33. Ibid., 107.

34. Ibid, 107–108.

35. Scrapbook 1, page 8A, The Mary Baker Eddy Collection.

36. *Retrospection and Introspection*, 30.

37. Ibid., 37.

38. Ibid., 34.

39. Ibid., 48–49.

40. *Miscellaneous Writings 1883–1896*, 308.

41. *Retrospection and Introspection*, 22.

42. Mary Baker Eddy did not name Josephine Woodbury outright as the "Babylonish woman," but Woodbury insisted that those present for the address knew it was a deliberate reference to her.

43. Frederick W. Peabody, *A Complete Exposé of Eddyism or Christian Science, and The Plain Truth in Plain Terms Regarding Mary Baker G. Eddy, Founder of Christian Science* (A pamphlet based on a lecture delivered at Tremont Temple, Boston, 1901), 13.

44. Ibid., 12, 58; *Footprints Fadeless*, 132.

45. See Peabody, *Complete Exposé*, 27, 39, 9; *Footprints Fadeless*, 129–131.

46. Frederick Peabody accused Mary Baker Eddy of allowing George Glover's remains to lie "with the unnumbered, unclaimed, and forgotten dead in the Potter's Field at Wilmington, N.C." See Peabody, *Complete Exposé*, 7. She, in contrast, explains that her husband was "buried with Masonic honors. A great procession followed his remains. His body was not allowed to be taken to our beautiful home in Charleston, owing to fear of contagion, but marked respect and affection were bestowed to his memory. The Wilmington city officials took possession of the body." *Footprints Fadeless*, 84–85. None of these funeral details are provided in *Retrospection and Introspection*.

47. Peabody argued that Eddy had "distinctly authorized the claim . . . that she herself was the chosen successor to and equal of Jesus." See Peabody, *Complete Exposé*, 21. In *Footprints Fadeless*, Eddy clarifies that she regarded "Christ as divine; and myself as a human being seeking Christ." *Footprints Fadeless*, 140.

48. Peabody, *Complete Exposé*, 62.

49. An unauthorized edition of *Footprints Fadeless* was published in the 1930s. Some copies are still extant. *Mary Baker Eddy, Speaking for Herself* contains the first *authorized* edition of *Footprints Fadeless* to ever appear in print.

50. Letter of Samuel J. Elder of Elder, Wait and Whitman to Judge Septimus Hanna of Boston, January 23, 1902. L09706, The Mary Baker Eddy Collection. Emphasis in original.

51. Ibid.

52. *Footprints Fadeless*, 106.

53. Ibid., 137.

54. Ibid., 140.

55. Ibid., 124.

56. Ibid., 127.

57. A10281, The Mary Baker Eddy Collection.

58. *Footprints Fadeless*, 106.

R ETROSPECTION AND I NTROSPECTION

59. Mary Baker Eddy was not related to Sir John Macneill, and this claim was attacked by a number of Eddy's critics during her lifetime. Eddy's cousin Fanny McNeil Potter mistakenly promoted the Macneill "connection."

60. Henry Moore Baker (1844–1912) of Bow, New Hampshire, was a member of the New Hampshire state senate, 1891–1892; a member of the U.S. House of Representatives from New Hampshire, 1893–1897; and a member of the New Hampshire state house of

representatives, 1905–1909; he was Mary Baker Eddy's cousin and legal counsel.

61. Lindley Murray (1745–1826), an American-born Quaker, retired around 1784 after a successful career as a lawyer and businessman in New York. He moved to England, where he wrote his famous *English Grammar* and other books. *English Grammar* ran into many editions. Used as a schoolbook in Great Britain, it was also translated into many different languages.

62. The Westminster Catechism (1647) refers to either of two works, the Larger Westminster Catechism and the Shorter Westminster Catechism, which have been used by English-speaking Presbyterians and by some Congregationalists and Baptists. Written in England by members of the Westminster Assembly, these manuals of religious instruction present questions followed by answers and are used to instruct the young, to win converts, and to testify to the faith.

63. See note 29.

64. The theologian John Calvin (1509–1564) wrote about the doctrine of predestination in his *Institutes of the Christian Religion* (1537). Briefly, this doctrine holds that God has foreknowledge of all that will happen and is wholly sovereign over creation. Calvin taught that all humans sin and deserve only condemnation, but God has pre-ordained, from the beginning of time, those whom He will graciously save—who, in Calvin's words, will be "favored with the government of His Spirit." Calvinists believe that we cannot understand why some are saved and others are not.

65. This statement appears to be based on the Annual Report of the Secretary of the Christian Scientist Association, read at its meeting of January 15, 1880. In this report, June is named as the month in which the charter was obtained, instead of August 23, 1879, the correct date.

66. Glover was actually a major, but "Colonel" was often used as a kind of honorary title in the South. Glover died on June 27, 1844, about six and a half months after he and Mary Baker were married. Their son was born on September 12, 1844, less than two months after her return to New Hampshire in late July.

67. Her son, George, almost twelve, was taken to Minnesota in April 1856, without her knowledge or permission. Mahala and Russell Cheney had been caring for George for the previous six years. Abigail Tilton had offered to take her sister into her home in 1850 but was unwilling to include George. The move of the Cheneys and George to Minnesota seems to have been engineered by her father, Mark Baker, and her second husband, Daniel Patterson, who evidently felt that the boy's rambunctious behavior served only to threaten his mother's precarious health. She would not hear from her son until 1861, and they did not meet again until 1879.

68. She obtained a divorce from Daniel Patterson on December 9, 1873, after twenty years of marriage.

69. Phineas Parkhurst Quimby (1802–1866) was a clockmaker, inventor, and daguerreotypist. In the late 1830s, he became an expert mesmerist (see note 75). He gave demonstrations of mesmerism and eventually developed a healing practice based on what might today be called "therapeutic touch" and mental suggestion; Mary Baker

Eddy consulted with Quimby in his office in Portland, Maine. Although he sometimes used religious language when talking with his patients, Quimby's treatments did not involve prayer.

70. From 1866 to 1869, Mary Baker Eddy explored the Old Testament book of Genesis in a lengthy manuscript titled "The Bible in Its Spiritual Meaning." Yet it was not until early 1872, after nearly six years of testing her findings in her practice of healing, that she began the actual writing of *Science and Health*. The first edition of Eddy's book was published in October 1875, and she spent the next thirty-five years refining its language through seven major revisions and more than four hundred editions.

71. The spiritualist movement began in 1848 in upstate New York with two sisters, Margaretta and Kate Fox. Mysterious rapping sounds occurred in the presence of the sisters, and many believed that these sounds were communications from spirits of the dead. Interest in spirit communication soon spread across the United States and into other countries. Adherents of spiritualism believed that mediums, or people sensitive to the spirit world, could facilitate communication with the dead, thereby proving the existence of life after death without reference to religious faith. By the 1880s, adherents of spiritualism numbered in the millions.

72. Homeopathy was founded by a German physician, Samuel Hahnemann (1755–1843), who believed that a disease could be cured by a diluted dose of the very substance or drug that would induce symptoms of the disease. According to homeopathy, the higher the dilution of a drug, the greater its potency. Sometime in the 1850s, Mary Baker Eddy cured a case of dropsy by going one step further—prescribing unmedicated pills. She began to think of disease as essen-

tially mental in nature when the woman who took this placebo was cured.

Hydropathy, or the "water cure," was based on the theory that pure water is the key to good health. Hydropathic treatment involved drinking plenty of pure water, as well as showering, bathing, or wrapping the body in wet bandages or sheets. At the height of the cure's popularity, more than 200 hydropathic institutes were in operation across the United States.

In the summer of 1862, at her sister Abigail's insistence, Mary Baker Eddy became a patient at Dr. William T. Vail's Hydropathic Institute at Hill, New Hampshire. The results of the treatment were unsatisfactory. As she remarked in a letter: "I have been at this Water Cure between 2 and 3 months, and when I came could walk ½ a mile, now I can sit up but a few minutes at one time." V03342, The Library of Congress, August 1862.

The Graham cure was developed by Sylvester Graham (1795–1851), an American Presbyterian minister who advocated various health practices including temperance, a vegetarian diet, and sexual abstinence. He recommended eating bread made from coarsely ground whole-wheat flour, which came to be known as graham bread. Thousands attended his lectures, and many boardinghouses and restaurants capitalized on his popularity by serving a Graham diet. As a young woman, Mary Baker Eddy adopted the Graham diet in an attempt to cure her digestive ailments.

73. "Jahr" refers to a popular manual listing homeopathic remedies and the symptoms they are said to relieve. The author, George Heinrich Gottlieb Jahr, worked with the founder of homeopathy, Samuel

Hahnemann, to prepare the *Manual of Homoeopathic Medicine* in 1834 and 1835.

74. *Natrum muriaticum* is a homeopathic remedy made from sea salt.

75. Franz Anton Mesmer (1734–1815), an Austrian physician widely acknowledged as the "Father of Hypnosis," believed that a magnetic fluid existed throughout the universe and was absorbed by the body's nerves. He thought disease was caused by blocked circulation of this magnetic fluid in the body; disease was cured by restoring its proper flow. Treatment of disease in this way, sometimes called animal magnetism, mesmerism, or (later) mental suggestion, was popular in nineteenth-century New England. Having been treated for her own ailments by Phineas Quimby (see note 69), whose practice had evolved from a background in mesmerism, Mary Baker Eddy eventually came to feel that mesmerism or animal magnetism could harm others by manipulating their minds. In fact, she ultimately used "animal magnetism" as a specific term for evil and its operations. Eddy referred to "mental malpractice" as the attempt of one individual to use mental means to harm another. But she also taught that the remedy for such malpractice was a consciousness of God's allness and goodness which would wipe out evil causes or effects, just as the presence of light dispels darkness.

76. See note 81.

77. Asa Gilbert Eddy was Mary Baker Eddy's third husband. The couple married on January 1, 1877—the bride age fifty-five, the groom approximately age forty-five. A former sewing machine salesman, Asa Eddy had joined the fledgling ranks of Christian Science in 1876 and

had a successful healing practice. Over the course of their five years together, he taught classes, served as publisher of the third edition of *Science and Health,* studied copyright law in order to defend his wife's writings from plagiarism, and showed steadfast loyalty to her during the defections of some of her followers and the criticism that outsiders sometimes directed toward the movement. Asa Gilbert Eddy died in 1882.

78. A homeopathic physician from Vermont, Ebenezer J. Foster Eddy (1847–1930) graduated from the Hahnemann Medical College in Philadelphia, Pennsylvania, in 1869. After a friend was healed by reading *Science and Health,* Dr. Foster entered one of Mary Baker Eddy's classes in 1887 and another in 1888. In November 1888, Eddy legally adopted him. He served as publisher of her writings from 1893 to 1896. Foster Eddy's persistent self-indulgence and disobedience, however, led to a permanent parting of ways in July 1897. In 1907 Foster Eddy joined forces with Mary Baker Eddy's biological son, George Glover, in the unsuccessful "Next Friends" suit. The two sons and other family members attempted to prove that she was mentally and physically unfit to manage her assets.

79. Originally a member of the Congregational Church, Calvin Frye (1845–1917) became interested in Christian Science after his mother, who suffered from insanity, was helped by one of Mary Baker Eddy's students. Eddy first taught him Christian Science in 1881 in Lynn, Massachusetts. He eventually took two more classes from her, and at the recommendation of her husband, Asa Gilbert Eddy, she selected Frye as her private secretary in 1882. A devoted employee and student, he held this position until Eddy's death in 1910.

80. Like most Christians of her era, Mary Baker Eddy believed that the

teachings of Jesus had succeeded those of Judaism as supreme religious truth. But unlike those who used (and still use) this viewpoint as an excuse for violent anti-Semitism, Eddy also respected Judaism, especially its monotheism, though her acquaintance with the faith was somewhat limited.

81. In 1880, Edward J. Arens, a former student of Asa Gilbert Eddy, published a pamphlet entitled *The Science of the Relation Between God and Man and the Distinction Between Spirit and Matter*. It was composed of nearly three hundred verbatim citations, used without attribution or permission, from Mary Baker Eddy's *The Science of Man* and *Science and Health*. Eddy sued Arens for plagiarism in April 1883 and won the case in September of that year. This lawsuit offers just one example of Eddy's efforts to maintain her place as the author of her own books. On the one hand, some wanted to add to or change her writings. Others took the position that women could not write intelligently about theology, metaphysics, medicine, and science, and claimed that her books were actually written by or derived from the works or thoughts of such men as Ralph Waldo Emerson, Phineas Quimby, philosopher G. W. F. Hegel, or even her editor, James Henry Wiggin.

FOOTPRINTS FADELESS

82. The earliest known published piece of writing attributed to Mary Baker Eddy appears in an 1840 issue of *Hills New Hampshire Patriot*. The earliest piece in the *Belknap Gazette* dates from 1842 (when she was twenty-one). In one document, Eddy refers to her first contributions to the *Belknap Gazette* as taking place at age fifteen; in an-

other letter she mentions age sixteen. It is possible that these earlier published writings exist but have not yet been found.

83. There is no solid evidence that Glover owned slaves, apart from Eddy's various assertions that he did. Probably Glover hired slaves on a temporary basis to do work at his business and his home—a common practice in the slaveholding South, particularly in urban areas.

84. Freemasonry is a society of men concerned with moral and spiritual values. Its members are taught its precepts by a series of ritual dramas, which follow ancient forms and use stonemasons' customs and tools as allegorical guides.

The essential qualification for admission and membership is belief in a Supreme Being. Membership is open to men of any race or religion who can fulfill this qualification and are of good repute. A Royal Arch Mason has taken degrees in that specific branch of Masonry. Women may become involved in auxiliary Masonic organizations.

85. "Citizen prisoner" indicates that Daniel Patterson was not part of the enlisted forces of the North. He was acting as a private citizen appointed by the governor of New Hampshire to bring money to Southerners loyal to the Union when he was captured by Confederate troops.

86. See note 69.

87. When Mary Baker Eddy quoted letters in her books or periodicals, she often edited them slightly for publication. Such is the case with this May 18, 1892, letter from Mary Philbrick, which was edited once for

The Christian Science Journal and once again for *Footprints Fadeless.*

88. A conspiracy charge was brought against Asa Gilbert Eddy and Edward J. Arens for the murder of Daniel Spofford on October 29, 1878. The charge was dismissed on January 31, 1879, after Daniel Spofford reappeared and several key witnesses recanted their testimony. Some contemporary scholars speculate that this complicated affair was most likely the result of a plot by Spofford and Richard Kennedy to disgrace the Eddys.

Daniel Spofford (1842–1924), a shoemaker in Lynn, Massachusetts, took a class in Mary Baker Eddy's healing method in April 1875. A year later, he took on the task of publishing and marketing her book. After her marriage to Asa Gilbert Eddy in January 1877, Spofford's relationship with his teacher and her new husband deteriorated, and he began to actively oppose her.

Richard Kennedy (1849–1921) first met Mary Baker Eddy in Amesbury, Massachusetts, and became her second student. In 1870, they both moved to Lynn and formed a partnership in which he paid her a portion of the income from his healing practice in exchange for her continued guidance of his work. The partnership was dissolved in 1872, when Kennedy rebelled against certain aspects of Christian Science teaching and began to oppose its founder.

For the rest of his life, Kennedy remained deeply hostile to Mary Baker Eddy and Christian Science. He developed mental problems in his later years and was committed to a Vermont insane asylum in 1918.

89. In an earlier letter to The Christian Science Board of Directors, dated December 19, 1894, Mary Baker Eddy explained her rationale: "The

Bible and *Science and Health with Key to the Scriptures* shall henceforth be the Pastor of the Mother Church. This will tend to spiritualize thought. Personal preaching has more or less of human views grafted into it. Whereas the pure Word contains only the living, health-giving Truth." L02748, The Mary Baker Eddy Collection.

90. Agamogenesis refers to asexual reproduction. Mary Baker Eddy's critic, Frederick Peabody, mocked the supposed (though nonexistent) Christian Science idea that spiritually advanced women could conceive children asexually. Peabody's accusation was probably designed as a subtle justification for why his former legal client, Josephine Woodbury, claimed she had immaculately conceived a child.

91. Mary Baker Eddy's final break with Foster Eddy came in 1897 (see note 78). There had definitely been quarrels between them prior to that time. The original letter from Foster Eddy to Eddy, dated October 22, 1901, has been carefully edited by her for inclusion in *Footprints Fadeless*. Some of the material she has removed from the letter is indicative of the earlier quarrels between them.

92. C.S.D., "Doctor of Christian Science," was a recognition generally awarded only by Mary Baker Eddy and reserved for those to whom she had taught Christian Science.

93. James Henry Wiggin (1836–1900), a Unitarian clergyman, retired from active ministry in 1875 to devote himself to writing and copy-editing. He assisted Mary Baker Eddy with the sixteenth and fiftieth editions of *Science and Health*. Wiggin also served as editor of *The Christian Science Journal* from January 1886 to January 1889 (with the exception of a few months in 1886).

94. For Mary Baker Eddy, part of the cost of being a successful and out-spoken woman was the unrelenting scrutiny of the American press. Such acclaim included negative publicity, suspicion, and doubt as to the validity of her leadership. As Eddy grew older, some members of the press questioned whether she was in good health, or even alive. These attacks culminated in the *New York World*'s sensational story of 1906: "Mrs. Mary Baker G. Eddy Dying; Footman and 'Dummy' Control Her." The story paved the way, in 1907, for an unsuccessful legal action against Eddy; relatives attempted to secure control of her person and property by claiming that she suffered from insane delusions.

95. Mary Baker Eddy's philanthropic activities were almost as varied as the needs of humanity itself. Her main expression of generosity involved healing, as shown in her treatment of a young minister who visited her in 1903, seeking a donation to repair the Methodist Church in Bow, New Hampshire. Not only did she double her donation but also healed Rev. E. N. Larmour of extreme nearsightedness; his vision remained perfect for the rest of his life. Eddy supported causes such as the Wendell Phillips Memorial and the Longfellow National Memorial, as well as educational initiatives such as a Dartmouth College building fund. Interestingly, she was not averse to giving to medical establishments, helping to fund a local hospital in 1908. When she resided in New Hampshire, she gave to a number of local causes, from the Concord YMCA and the New Hampshire Historical Society building fund to the New Hampshire state exhibit at the St. Louis Exposition of 1904. Eddy responded to disaster victims after earthquakes devastated San Francisco in 1906 and Messina, Sicily, in 1908, and she sent money when catastrophe struck closer to home, helping to replace a building de-

stroyed by fire at the Canterbury Shaker village in southern New Hampshire.

96. The statement "over a million Christian Scientists" does not give the number of those who were members of The First Church of Christ, Scientist, at this time, but may refer to the number of individuals studying *Science and Health* and attending church services.

HIGHLIGHTS FROM
THE LIFE OF MARY BAKER EDDY

1821   Mary Morse Baker born on a farm in Bow, New Hampshire, youngest of the six children of Mark Baker and Abigail Ambrose Baker.

1829   Mary Baker hears her name being called by an unseen voice. Recurs over a 12-month period.

1836   Bakers move to new farm near Sanbornton Bridge (now Tilton), New Hampshire.

1838   Joins the Congregational Church in Sanbornton Bridge, New Hampshire.

1841   Favorite brother, Albert Baker, dies at age 31.

1843   Mary Baker, 22, marries George Washington Glover, 32, a building contractor. The couple moves to the Carolinas.

1844   George Glover dies. Pregnant and in difficult financial straits, Mary Glover returns to her parents' home and gives birth to her first and only child, George Washington Glover II.

1846   Runs experimental kindergarten school in Sanbornton.

Offered salary of $3,000 by *Odd Fellows'* magazine for regular contributions.

1849   Mother, Abigail Ambrose Baker, dies.

John Harriman Bartlett, to whom Mary Glover is betrothed, dies.

1850   Father Mark Baker marries Elizabeth Patterson Duncan.

1851   Sister, Abigail Tilton, offers Mary Glover a home, but son George is not welcome. George is sent to live in North Groton, New Hampshire, with Mahala and Russell Cheney. Mary writes poem "The Mother at Parting with her Child."

1853   Mary Glover marries dentist and homeopath Daniel Patterson and moves to Franklin, New Hampshire.

1855   The Pattersons move to North Groton, New Hampshire, to be near son George.

CONTEMPORARY AMERICAN EVENTS

1820   James Monroe is elected to a second term as president.

1825   John Quincy Adams is elected president.

Homeopathic medicine comes to the United States.

Erie Canal completed.

1830   The Church of Latter-day Saints is incorporated. In 1838 it is renamed The Church of Jesus Christ of Latter-day Saints.

1831   William Lloyd Garrison publishes the first issue of the antislavery journal *The Liberator.*

1833   American Anti-Slavery Society founded.

Oberlin College opens, coed.

1835   Samuel Morse invents the telegraph.

James Gordon Bennett publishes the *New York Herald,* the first penny paper— helps to distribute the news more broadly.

Sarah Josepha Hale becomes editor of *Godey's Lady's Book.*

1836–1837 Grimké sisters publish lecture on opposing slavery, supporting women's rights.

1838   Transcendentalist Ralph Waldo Emerson addresses Harvard Divinity School.

1838–1839 The Cherokees are forced by the U.S. government to leave their homes in Georgia and march to Indian territory (present-day Oklahoma). One quarter of the population dies on what is known as the "Trail of Tears."

1840   33% of American people now located west of Appalachians.

1841   Dorothea Dix begins crusade for better treatment of mentally ill.

1856   Son George, almost 12 years old, is taken to Minnesota by the Cheneys. Hears from George in 1861, but does not see him again until 1879.

Mary Patterson is bedridden for most of the next six years.

1862   At sister Abigail's initiative, Mary Patterson goes to Dr. W. T. Vail's Hydropathic Institute at Hill, New Hampshire, seeking a cure. She stays about three months.

Mary Patterson visits Dr. Phineas P. Quimby for the first time at his office in the International Hotel, Portland, Maine. Remains in Portland for the rest of the year, boarding at the home of Mrs. Hunter on Chestnut Street.

1865   Now living in Lynn, Massachusetts, she becomes active in the temperance movement.

Father, Mark Baker, dies.

1866   January 16: Phineas Parkhurst Quimby dies in Belfast, Maine.

February 1: Mary Patterson falls on an icy sidewalk and is seriously injured.

February 4: Reads New Testament accounts of Jesus' healings and is healed of her injuries—discovery of Christian Science.

August: Daniel Patterson's desertion of his wife.

Autumn: Begins notes on Genesis. Writes hundreds of pages of biblical exposition (1866–1869) in a manuscript titled "The Bible in Its Spiritual Meaning."

1867   Teaches her first student, Hiram Crafts.

1868   Called to heal Mrs. Mary Gale in Manchester, New Hampshire, who was dying of pneumonia caused by consumption. The doctor in attendance informs her that there is no hope for the patient. She cures the woman and the doctor urges her to write a book about her system of healing.

1870   Settles in the area of Lynn, Massachusetts, for 12 years, often changing residence.

Begins teaching classes on Christian Science and maintains a healing practice.

1872   Begins actual writing of *Science and Health*. Her first working title for the book is *The Science of Life*.

1841   Three Oberlin students become the first women to receive U.S. college degrees.

1844   Members of the Millerite sect expect the Second Coming of Christ on October 22.

Samuel Morse perfects the telegraph for practical use.

1845   Famine in Ireland brings Catholic immigrants to United States.

U.S. annexation of Texas.

1846–1848   Mexican War.

1847   American Medical Association founded.

1848   United States acquires Southwest and California from Mexico.

The spiritualist movement is born with the activities of the Fox Sisters in New York State.

First Woman's Rights Convention, Seneca Falls, New York.

1849   Elizabeth Blackwell graduates from Geneva Medical College, becoming the first woman to earn an M.D. degree.

California Gold Rush begins.

1850   Fugitive Slave Act makes it the responsibility of the federal government to return runaway slaves.

Harriet Tubman, runaway slave, makes her first trip back to the South to rescue others. In ten years she rescues 200–300 from slavery.

1852   Harriet Beecher Stowe publishes *Uncle Tom's Cabin*.

Rebecca Pennell becomes first U.S. woman professor—Antioch College.

1853   Antoinette Brown Blackwell ordained by her congregation.

1873   After 20 years of marriage, wins divorce from Daniel Patterson on grounds of desertion.

1875   Publishes the first edition of *Science and Health* on October 30.

1876   Heals Asa Gilbert Eddy of a heart condition. He studies with her and becomes a Christian Science practitioner within four weeks.

Organizes the Christian Scientist Association of her pupils.

1877   Marries third husband, Asa Gilbert Eddy.

1878   November: Begins to preach a series of Sunday afternoon sermons in vestry of Tabernacle Baptist Church in Boston. Last sermon in this church is February 2, 1879.

A conspiracy charge is brought against Asa Gilbert Eddy and Edward J. Arens for the murder of Daniel Spofford on October 29. The charge is dismissed on January 31, 1879.

1879   The Christian Scientist Association forms the Church of Christ (Scientist).

1880   Publishes her sermon *Christian Healing*.

1881   Obtains charter for the Massachusetts Metaphysical College, to teach courses on spiritual healing.

Mary Baker Eddy ordained pastor by her church.

1882   The Eddys move from Lynn to Boston.

Asa Gilbert Eddy dies.

1883   Launches the *Journal of Christian Science* (later renamed *The Christian Science Journal*).

Publishes *The People's God: Its Effect on Health and Christianity* (later *The People's Idea of God: Its Effect on Health and Christianity*).

Brings suit against Edward J. Arens for infringement of copyright and wins.

1885   Publishes *Historical Sketch of Metaphysical Healing* (later *Retrospection and Introspection*).

1887   Publishes *Christian Science: No and Yes* (later retitled *No and Yes*).

1854   Kansas and Nebraska territories organized, introducing popular sovereignty in territories on the issue of slavery.

Massachusetts Married Women's Property Act allows wives to control their own property and make wills. They soon gain equal rights to guardianship of children.

1854–1855   An ongoing campaign of war by the U.S. government against many Plains Native American nations begins in what has been called the Grattan Massacre and the Battle of Blue Water in Nebraska Territory.

1857   Dred Scott decision declares that slaves are not citizens of the United States, and cannot sue in federal courts; that Congress does not have the power to prohibit slavery in a territory.

1859   Charles Darwin publishes *On the Origin of Species by Means of Natural Selection*.

1860   Abraham Lincoln is elected president.

Pony Express starts.

1861   South Carolina's attack on Fort Sumter ignites the Civil War.

1863   President Lincoln's Emancipation Proclamation takes effect, freeing slaves in areas not under Union control.

Seventh-day Adventist church is officially organized with Ellen Gould White as the principal founder.

Olympia Brown becomes first woman ordained by her denomination.

1865   Civil War ends.

President Lincoln is assassinated on April 14.

Thirteenth Amendment, abolishing slavery, is ratified.

1887   Publishes *Rudiments and Rules of Divine Science* (later *Rudimental Divine Science*).

1888   Publishes *Unity of Good and Unreality of Evil* (later retitled *Unity of Good*).

Adopts Ebenezer J. Foster as her son.

1889   Moves from Boston to Concord, New Hampshire, dissolves The Christian Scientist Association, closes the Massachusetts Metaphysical College, and formally disorganizes the church.

1890   Publishes *Christian Science Quarterly*—Bible Lessons.

1891   Publishes landmark 50th edition of *Science and Health*. A reordering of the chapters, new chapter titles, and the addition of marginal headings make this the first edition to contain many elements familiar to readers today.

Publishes *Retrospection and Introspection*.

1892   Reorganizes Church of Christ (Scientist) as The First Church of Christ, Scientist, in Boston, Massachusetts, and establishes a Board of Directors.

1893   Publishes *Christ and Christmas*.

Moves to "Pleasant View," home in Concord, New Hampshire.

1894   Ordains the Bible and *Science and Health* as pastor of The Mother Church.

1895   Dedication of the Original Edifice of The Mother Church.

Ordains Bible and *Science and Health* as pastor for all branch churches.

Publishes *Pulpit and Press* and *Manual of The Mother Church*.

1897   Breaks all ties with Ebenezer Foster Eddy.

Publishes *Miscellaneous Writings 1883–1896*.

1898   Establishes the Board of Lectureship, The Christian Science Publishing Society, the Board of Education, and the Committee on Publication as part of The First Church of Christ, Scientist.

First issue of *Christian Science Weekly* (later renamed *Christian Science Sentinel*) is published.

1867   Alaska purchased.

1868   Fourteenth Amendment ratified, guaranteeing the basic civil rights of all citizens.

1869   Transcontinental railroad is completed.

1870   Fifteenth Amendment prohibits the denial of voting rights to male citizens on the basis of race, color, or previous servitude.

1873   The Panic of 1873 begins a five-year economic depression.

1874   Women's Christian Temperance Union is founded to address the problems of alcohol abuse in families and society.

1876   Alexander Graham Bell invents the telephone.

Centennial Exposition in Philadelphia celebrates the nation's 100th birthday with displays of art, international culture, American inventions, and other aspects of American life.

Julia Smith publishes translation of the Bible.

1879   Thomas Edison invents the first practical lightbulb.

1881   President James A. Garfield is assassinated.

Clara Barton founds the American Red Cross.

1882   Women's National Press Association formed.

1883   Joseph Pulitzer buys *New York World*.

1885   U.S. population reaches 50 million.

1889   North Dakota, South Dakota, Montana, and Washington become states (42 total).

1890   Wyoming becomes the first state where women can vote.

1898   Publishes *Christian Science versus Pantheism*.

   Teaches last class in Concord, New Hampshire.

1901   Frederick W. Peabody gives a lecture in Tremont Temple, Boston, attacking Mrs. Eddy. He publishes the lecture as a pamphlet entitled *A Complete Exposé of Eddyism or Christian Science, and The Plain Truth in Plain Terms Regarding Mary Baker G. Eddy, Founder of Christian Science*.

1902   Publishes revised and essentially definitive (226th) edition of *Science and Health*. Adds new chapter, "Fruitage," to include people's accounts of being healed by reading her book.

   Completes a draft of *Footprints Fadeless* but is discouraged from publishing it.

1903   Establishes the *Herald of Christian Science* with the German publication *Der Christian Science Herold*.

1907   Suit on "behalf" of Mary Baker Eddy, alleging misuse of her property and abuse of her person, is filed against church officials and others by her "next friends," including George W. Glover II (her son), George W. Baker (her nephew), and Ebenezer J. Foster Eddy (her adopted son). Suit is unsuccessful.

1908   Moves to Chestnut Hill, Boston.

   Publishes first issue of *The Christian Science Monitor*.

1910   Authorizes work on a German translation of *Science and Health*, which is published in 1912. *Science and Health* is translated into an additional fifteen languages over the next seven decades.

   Mary Baker Eddy dies at her home in Chestnut Hill, Boston, at the age of 89. Her last written words are "God is my life."

1890   Wounded Knee Massacre in South Dakota kills over 150 Lakota Sioux.

1892   Ellis Island, in New York City's harbor, opens as station for U.S. immigration.

1893   Chicago World's Fair.

1895   Elizabeth Cady Stanton publishes *The Woman's Bible.*

1897   Klondike Gold Rush begins.

1898   Spanish American War.

1901   President William McKinley is assassinated—Vice President Theodore Roosevelt succeeds him.

1903   At Kitty Hawk, North Carolina, Orville Wright flies the first successful airplane.

1908   Henry Ford revolutionizes the automobile industry by developing the first mass-produced car, the Model T.

1910   Flexner report critiques medical schools and recommends establishment of fixed standards for medical education and training.

1914–1918 World War I.

1920   The Nineteenth Amendment is ratified, granting women the right to vote.

INDEX

F OR MORE INFORMATION. . .

www.marybakereddylibrary.org offers an in-depth look at Mary Baker Eddy's life and legacy. The Mary Baker Eddy Library for the Betterment of Humanity houses The Mary Baker Eddy Collection™—one of the largest by and about an American woman—which includes thousands of pages of Eddy's letters, diaries, and manuscripts, as well as photographs, artifacts, and historic homes. The website features upcoming events, forums, research programs, summer institutes, and online exhibits, all inspired by Eddy's timeless ideas and life of achievement.

www.spirituality.com is a dynamic website based on the ideas in Eddy's bestselling work, *Science and Health with Key to the Scriptures*. Articles, features, discussion boards, and live round-table chats explore spirituality in relation to careers, finance, self/identity, wellness, relationships, and more. The full texts of *Science and Health* and Eddy's autobiography *Retrospection and Introspection* are searchable online, and users can sign up for daily inspirational e-mails, maintain a private online journal, and contribute their own content to the site. There's also a Writers' Corner and an interactive kids' section, spirituality.kids.

CCI0209036A

Christian S[c]

[b]ook of the

[w]hich indic[a]

[a]natines fro[m]

the flexibil[i]

[o]pposite of

magnetism